AFRICAN AMERICANS
IN
FLORIDA

M000276585

AFRICAN AMERICANS IN FLORIDA

MAXINE D. JONES AND KEVIN M. McCARTHY

PINEAPPLE PRESS, INC.
SARASOTA, FLORIDA

AFRICAN AMERICANS
IN
FLORIDA

PINEAPPLE PRESS, INC.
P.O. DRAWER 16008
SOUTHSIDE STATION
SARASOTA, FLORIDA 34239

Library of Congress Cataloging-in-Publication Data

Jones, Maxine.
African Americans in Florida: an illustrated history / Maxine D. Jones and Kevin M. McCarthy – 1st ed.
p. cm.
Includes bibliographical references and index.
Summary: Briefly describes the lives and contributions of more than 50 notable African Americans in Florida, from 1528 to the present, in such fields as education, politics, journalism, sports, music and religion.
ISBN 1-56164-030-1 : $24.95. – ISBN 1-56164-031-X (pbk.) : $17.95
1. Afro-Americans–Florida–History–Juvenile literature. 2. Afro-Americans–Florida–History–Pictorial works-Juvenile literature. 3. Florida–History–Juvenile literature. 4. Florida–History–Pictorial Works-Juvenile literature. [1. Afro-Americans–Florida–History. 2. Afro-Americans–Florida–Biography. 3. Florida–History. 4. Florida–Biography.] I. McCarthy, Kevin M.. II. Title
E185.93.F5M37 1993
975.9 ' 00496073–dc20   93-27737
                                       CIP
                                       AC

FIRST EDITION
10 9 8 7 6 5 4 3 2 1

DESIGN AND COMPOSITION BY
ROBERT FLEURY

FOREWORD

ON THE AFTERNOON OF MAY 27, 1956, two young African American women stepped onto a bus in Tallahassee, Florida. They paid their fare, turned to find some empty seats, and found that only two were unoccupied. So they sat down in those places. The problem was that those two seats were in the "whites only" section. When the bus driver ordered them to get up and go stand in the "colored" section, they refused. They were tired, there were two available seats on the bus, and they saw no reason to give those places up. The time had come to take a stand. In the words of countless people around the world who were tired of being discriminated against, "Enough is enough! Segregation is wrong, and it has got to stop."

That spring afternoon was 428 years after the first African had stepped ashore with the early Spanish explorers. It was 200 years after runaway slaves fled South Carolina plantations for the freedom of Florida. It was 92 years after African American soldiers had fought Southerners at the Battle of Olustee in the Civil War, a war that freed slaves throughout the South.

The struggle that began in Tallahassee that afternoon in 1956 continues to the present day as African Americans and whites try to establish a color-blind state, a society that does not judge people by the color of their skin. That struggle will continue long after all of us are gone from this earth. But it will go on.

Just as it has gone on for the past four centuries. This book tells the story of those 400 years—the ups and downs, the steps forward and the steps backward, the progress made and the reversals suffered. We write this introduction in 1993 on the birthday of Dr. Martin Luther King, Jr., a great American and one who came to Florida to help integrate its society in the 1960s. Has that society succeeded in integrating itself? This is a question we hope one can answer by reading this book.

This book's writers come to this project with different backgrounds. One is African American; the other is white. One is a woman; the other is a man. One is from the South; the other is from the North. One teaches in a Department of History; the other teaches in a Department of English. Together they paint the picture of what Florida has meant to the African American all these years. If it is not a completely pretty picture, it does have its heroes of both races, its hopeful signs, the proud accomplishments of thousands of African Americans who have called Florida home.

May all who read these pages come away with a better understanding of how much the African Americans of Florida have endured and the contributions they have made to Florida's history. It is also our hope that readers get a sense of how far we still have to go to make our state and our society truly color-blind.

Maxine D. Jones
    Department of History
    Florida State University
    Tallahassee, Florida

Kevin M. McCarthy
    Department of English
    University of Florida
    Gainesville, Florida

TABLE OF

CONTENTS

1.
ESTEVANICO THE BLACK, 1528

Timucuan Native Americans trapping fish, 1562
Florida State Archives

NATIVE AMERICANS had lived in Florida for about 12,000 years before European explorers reached its shores in 1513. Spanish explorer Ponce de Léon arrived that year and named the land **"Pascua Florida,"** which means "feast of flowers" in Spanish. Another Spanish explorer, Panfilo de Narváez, arrived in April 1528 and began a long inland trip with about 300 men from **Tampa Bay** up toward present-day **Tallahassee**. One of the men who went along with him was Estevanico the Black, a man from the west coast of **Morocco** in Africa.

Estevanico, who was born sometime before 1500, was captured by Spanish soldiers in 1513 in Africa and became a **slave** for a Spanish nobleman. In 1528, he and his master joined the great Spanish explorer Panfilo de Narváez. They sailed to Florida and landed near present-day **St. Petersburg** around April 16, 1528.

That was the beginning of an eight-year journey that would take Estevanico up

DISCUSSION TOPICS: As you read this chapter, think about the answers to these questions: 1. Do you think the Spanish phrase "Pascua Florida" is a good name for our state? Why or why not? 2. What materials would the Spanish explorers need to build a raft to use on the sea? 3. How do you think the Native Americans used the fish trap pictured in the sketch?

> *VOCABULARY*
> Pascua Florida, Tampa Bay, Tallahassee, Morocco, slave, St. Petersburg

through Florida and on to Arizona and Mexico. In Florida he showed great skill in talking with the Native Americans that the Spanish explorers met along the way. The Spanish were looking for gold on that long journey. The Native Americans did not trust these strange men and attacked them along the way. Even though the Spanish soldiers wore thick armor to protect themselves, the arrows of the Native Americans went through the armor or found unprotected places.

Panfilo de Narváez
Florida State Archives

Further reading:
J. Norman Heard, *The Black Frontiersmen: Adventures of Negroes Among American Native Americans, 1528-1918* (New York: The John Day Company, 1969); John Upton Terrell, *Estevanico the Black* (Los Angeles, CA: Westernlore Press, 1968).

Also, the heat, millions of bugs, and deep swamps made the trip terribly hard.

When Narvez's troops, or what was left of them, reached the Gulf of Mexico below present-day Tallahassee, they were too tired to continue fighting the Native Americans. By that time the Spanish wanted to escape to friendlier lands. They decided to build rafts to get away from the Native Americans. But even then, the Spanish had terrible problems. Storms pushed several of the rafts out to sea, and many of the men drowned. Estevanico's raft was blown westward and eventually reached a place called La Isla de Mal Hado (Bad Luck Island) near present-day Galveston, Texas.

There Estevanico and his companions went on land, where they met another group of Native Americans. This time, however, the Native Americans took pity on the tired and hungry Spanish soldiers and did not attack them. Many of the Spanish had died because of battles with Native Americans, shipwreck, and disease. A small group of them, including Estevanico, finally reached Mexico after walking for more than 3,000 miles.

Instead of returning to Europe, Estevanico did more exploring in lands that Europeans and Africans had never seen before. Although he had survived many, many dangers in his travels, he finally reached the end of his life when he entered a Native American village in New Mexico. For some unknown reason, the Native Americans suspected that he was a spy for an army of soldiers following him and killed him.

Estevanico won much praise from those he had worked with. He was the first African to travel through Florida and much of the southwestern part of the present-day United States, and he led the way for others to settle those lands.

2.

SLAVE SHIPS, 1700

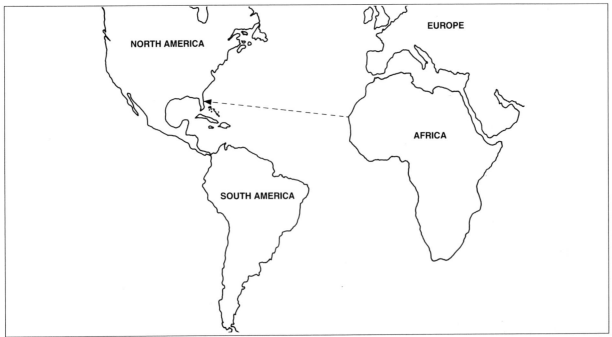

Slaves were taken from Africa to Florida.

FOR MANY YEARS AFTER THE VOYAGES of Christopher Columbus to the New World and after the Spanish began to establish settlements in Florida, the Spanish used Native Americans as slaves. But many Native Americans died from European diseases. And Catholic **missionaries** believed that the Spanish should try to **convert** the Native Americans. Therefore the Spanish needed another source of cheap labor. They looked to Africa for that labor.

Beginning in the mid-1400s, even before Columbus reached the New World, European nations like Portugal and Spain had gone to Africa to capture Africans for the slave trade. England, Holland, and France, as well as the United States, also joined in that slave trade, capturing Africans and taking them by ship to **plantations** around the world. Slave traders would put the slaves, including men, women, and children, into chains and march them long distances to the coast. Then they would put them on board ships for the long trip, often across the Atlantic Ocean.

The trip across the Atlantic was a terrible one for the slaves. In order to put as many slaves as possible into the ships, the sailors would force hundreds of Africans into a small space below decks. The space be-

DISCUSSION TOPICS: As you read this chapter, think about the answers to these questions: 1. Why did the Spanish decide to use African slaves instead of Native Americans on plantations? 2. Why did so many slaves die during the passage from Africa to America? 3. What is the purpose of placing a stone marker at the place of a shipwreck like the *Henrietta Marie* in the Florida Keys?

VOCABULARY
missionaries, convert, plantations, Brazil, Jamaica, shackles, reef, memorial

tween the floor and ceiling was as little as four feet, which did not allow the slaves to stand up. When the weather became stormy, the crews might close the windows that allowed fresh air into the area where the slaves were held. The closing of those windows would cause sickness among the slaves, and even more slaves died.

The slaves were forced to stay in their tiny spaces for at least five weeks, sometimes as long as eight. It all depended on the winds taking the ship across the Atlantic. Sometimes the crews would allow women and children to stay on the deck, which would open up more space below decks for more men slaves. It is no wonder that half of the slaves that began the trip in Africa died before they reached South America or North America.

We do not know exactly how many Africans were forced to make that terrible trip across the Atlantic. Some writers think that between 20 million and 50 million Africans were taken from Africa, but many of them died during the crossing and were buried (dropped overboard) at sea.

While many slave ships stopped in **Brazil** or **Jamaica** to put their slaves to work on the plantations there, some ships made it to Florida. The discovery of a shipwreck in the ocean near south Florida that used to be a slave ship tells us that slave ships passed along Florida on their way back to Europe. One such ship was the *Henrietta Marie*, a slave ship that sank near Key West around 1701. Divers found many sets of iron leg **shackles** and wrist shackles that slave traders used on the slaves to keep them from moving too much on the ship.

When a ship like the *Henrietta Marie* hit a **reef** off the Florida coast and began to sink, the crew would leave the ship and try to reach the shore. The slaves on board would be left behind to drown below decks. It must have been a terrible death for the slaves who were locked up below decks.

Slave ships like the *Henrietta Marie* could carry as many as 400 slaves. A slave trader could buy a slave in Africa for a small amount of money and then sell that same slave for $200 in South America or the United States. That meant a lot of money for the slave traders. The United States tried to end the slave trade around 1807, but many slave traders could not be stopped.

In 1993, the National Association of Black Scuba Divers placed a **memorial** to the many African slaves who suffered so much or died during the crossing of the Atlantic Ocean in the slave ships.

Slaves on the *Wildfire*, which was brought into Key West in 1860.

P.K. Yonge Library of Florida History, University of Florida

Further reading:
Herbert S. Klein, *The Middle Passage* (Princeton: Princeton University Press, 1978); Daniel P. Mannix, *Black Cargoes: A History of the Atlantic Slave Trade, 1518-1865* (New York: Viking, 1962); Kevin M. McCarthy, "Henrietta Marie," in *Thirty Florida Ship- wrecks* (Sarasota: Pineapple Press, 1992), pp. 28-31.

3.

FORT MOSE, 1738

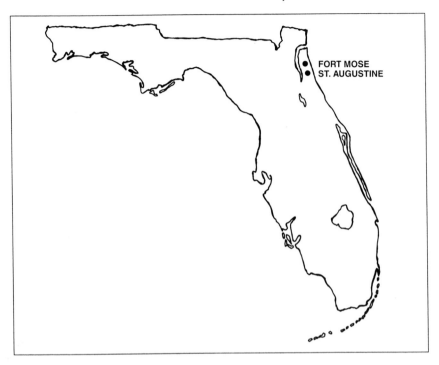

FORT MOSE
ST. AUGUSTINE

JUST NORTH OF ST. AUGUSTINE was a place where slaves escaping from Georgia and South Carolina found safety. Beginning in 1687, slaves began arriving in north Florida from Georgia. They were escaping from the British, who controlled Georgia. The Spanish controlled Florida. In 1738, the Spanish established Fort Mose (pronounced "Moh-say") two miles north of St. Augustine and allowed escaping slaves to settle there if they became Catholics. That fort became the first free black community in North America. About 100 free black men, women, and children lived at the fort, farmed the fields, and helped defend St. Augustine from the British.

DISCUSSION TOPICS: As you read this chapter, think about the answers to these questions: 1. Why did runaway slaves from Georgia go to Florida? 2. What do you think would happen to the runaway slaves in Florida if the British recaptured them? 3. Do you think that the state of Florida should make Fort Mose a memorial to African Americans? Why?

In 1740, when the British attacked St. Augustine, Fort Mose was destroyed. The Spanish, helped by the black soldiers of Fort Mose, beat back the British and saved St. Augustine. One reason the people of Fort Mose fought so hard was that they knew, if the British captured them, the British would make them slaves again.

For the next 12 years Fort Mose was not used, and the free blacks lived in St. Augustine with the Spanish. As more and more slaves escaped from Georgia and South Carolina and came south to Florida, Spanish **officials** decided to build Fort Mose again. In 1752, workers rebuilt the fort a little bit farther north than the original fort. The fort had three protected sides, while the side facing the river was open.

> *VOCABULARY*
> officials, carpenters, ironsmiths,
> Florida Black Heritage Trail

13

Florida in 1750
Florida State Archives

In 1759, 67 African Americans lived at Fort Mose: 37 men, 15 women, 7 boys, and 8 girls. The former slaves at Fort Mose knew the area well. They knew the plants which they could use as medicine, how to round up wild cattle and horses, and where to find food. They were also good hunters and guides for the Spanish. The place had a large Catholic church where the people prayed, and a Catholic priest helped teach the people. They farmed for a living, but Native American attacks made that dangerous. The men also worked as **carpenters** and **ironsmiths**. The women raised vegetables, chickens, and pigs, and also baked, cooked, washed, and sewed clothes. Like the Native Americans in the area, the people at Fort Mose ate fish, turtles, raccoons, opossums, and deer.

The African American soldiers at Fort Mose continued to value freedom and risked their lives in fighting for it. Finally, in 1763, when the British took control of Florida, the African Americans abandoned Fort Mose and went with the Spanish of St. Augustine to Cuba to begin new lives.

Fort Mose is part of something called the **Florida Black Heritage Trail**. The Trail is a list of 141 places around the state that are of importance in the history of African Ameri-

cans in Florida. Fort Mose is a proud memorial to African Americans who had escaped slavery in Georgia and South Carolina and came to Florida. They risked their lives to find a free life near St. Augustine and begin to raise their families with hope for the future.

Fort Mose will be a great memorial to how strongly those African Americans felt about freedom 250 years ago. The state of Florida owns the place where the fort was and may make a permanent display of a part of Florida history that African Americans, and indeed all free people, can look upon with pride. Those early African Americans risked, and sometimes lost, their lives in the struggle to gain freedom, a struggle that has continued to this day in America.

Further reading:
Betty Dunckel Camp, Fort Mose Educational Packet and video available for sale from the Collectors Shop at the Florida Museum of Natural History, University of Florida, Gainesville, FL 32611; Kathleen A. Deagan, "Fort Mose: America's First Free Black Community," in *Spanish Pathways in Florida* edited by Ann L. Henderson and Gary Mormino (Sarasota: Pineapple Press, 1991).

4.

THE NEGRO FORT, 1816

SIX YEARS BEFORE THE UNITED STATES took control of Florida from Spain, many African Americans were living in west Florida. They were runaway slaves or men and women who had once been slaves. What they wanted in Florida was freedom. The African Americans were living at a fort in a place called Prospect Bluff on the **Apalachicola River** 15 miles from the Gulf of Mexico. The English had built that fort and then turned it over to the African Americans and Native Americans living there.

The leader of the African Americans was a man named Garcon or Garcia. He had gathered over 300 African Americans to live in and near the place, which was then called the Negro Fort. Farmers and planters who lived north of there were worried that the Negro Fort would control the Apalachicola River and maybe stop the ships going up and down the river. General **Andrew Jackson**, who would later become president of the United States, ordered his troops to destroy the fort and return the African Americans to their owners.

In 1816 two Navy **gunboats** sailed up the river to attack. When these forces fired their guns, one of their **cannonballs** landed in a room full of ammunition and blew up the fort. In the explosion, over 200 men, women, and children inside were killed, and most of the 100 survivors were badly wounded. Garcon was captured by the federal troops and shot to death.

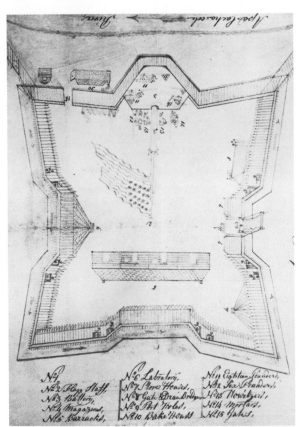

The Negro Fort
Florida State Archives

DISCUSSION TOPICS: As you read this chapter, think about the answers to these questions: 1. Why did runaway slaves go to Florida? 2. What did white farmers and planters who lived north of the Negro Fort worry about? 3. Why do you think the Spanish were not able to control Florida?

VOCABULARY
Apalachicola River, Andrew Jackson, gunboats, cannonballs

Andrew Jackson
Dictionary of American Portraits

The destruction of the fort put an end to the dreams of those 300 African Americans who had hoped to find freedom in north Florida. The incident also made Americans aware that the Spanish, who controlled Florida, were not able to keep order within its borders. Many Americans began wanting the United States to take control of Florida, which happened in 1821.

Further reading:

William Loren Katz. *Eyewitness: The Negro in American History* (Belmont, CA: Pitman Publishing Corporation), pp. 82-84.

General Andrew Jackson, who would later be president of the United States, wrote the following about the Negro Fort:

I have little doubt of the fact, that this fort has been established by some villains for the purpose of rapine [seizing and carrying away] and plunder, and that it ought to be blown up, regardless of the ground on which it stands; and if your mind shall have formed the same conclusion, destroy it and return the stolen Negroes and property to their rightful owners.

16

5.

ZEPHANIAH KINGSLEY'S PLANTATION, 1820

Kingsley Home
Kevin M. McCarthy

A WHITE CHILD by the name of Zephaniah Kingsley was born in Scotland on December 4, 1765. When he grew up, he spent much time in the slave trade business, buying and selling slaves in Africa, Brazil, and the West Indies. In 1803, he came to Florida and later settled down on Fort George Island above Jacksonville. There he began bringing in slaves from Africa. He planned to **smuggle** them across the border into Georgia and the rest of the United States. The United States did not allow anyone to bring in slaves after 1808. But Florida still belonged to Spain, and so **smugglers** brought in slaves to the southern United States through northern Florida.

Many of the 250,000 Africans who were sold into slavery in the South were brought in through Florida, because Florida had such a long coast and so many hidden places along the shore where ships from Africa could unload their slaves. The United States took control of Florida in 1821, but smugglers continued to bring in slaves.

Kingsley wanted to do more than just sell the slaves as **unskilled workers** to work on Southern plantations. He wanted to train

---

DISCUSSION TOPICS: As you read this chapter, think about the answers to these questions: 1. Why was Fort George Island a good place for smugglers to use for smuggling slaves into the United States? 2. Why did Zephaniah Kingsley train his slaves to be skilled workers? 3. Do you think Zephaniah Kingsley was right in training his slaves to be skilled workers?

> *VOCABULARY*
> smuggle, smugglers, unskilled workers,
> Madagascar, Haiti, will

Slave cabins on the Kingsley Plantation
Kevin M. McCarthy

them as skilled workers. Then he could sell them in other Southern states for high prices. He married one of the women slaves, a beautiful African woman whose father may have been a chief on the island of **Madagascar** in Africa. Kingsley described her as "very capable, and could carry on all the affairs of the plantation in my absence, as well as I could myself. She was affectionate and faithful, and I could trust her."

After the United States took control of Florida in 1821, Kingsley stopped smuggling slaves into Georgia. He began arguing that we should treat African Americans better. In the remaining years of his life, he set up a colony in the country of **Haiti** where people who had been slaves would be free. He sent some of his own slaves there as free people. He might have been more successful in setting up that colony, but very cold weather

killed off many of the orange trees on his Florida plantation, and he did not have the money he needed for the Haiti colony.

Kingsley died in 1843. He had made a **will** in which he wanted to give his African wife the land and buildings he had. His niece did not like that idea and tried to stop it. The niece argued that Kingsley's wife was a slave and therefore should not receive any property. Later a court decided that Kingsley's African wife could receive the land and buildings.

Today visitors can visit the Kingsley Plantation off highway A1A above Jacksonville. That place is the oldest plantation house in Florida and one of the few examples of what plantation life was like. This important place is Number 49 on the Florida Black Heritage Trail.

Descendants of slaves near slave quarters on Kingsley Plantation
Florida State Archives

Further reading:
Charles E. Bennett, *Twelve on the River St. Johns*
(Jacksonville: University of North Florida Press, 1980),
pp. 89-113.

19

6

AFRICAN AMERICANS IN SOUTH FLORIDA

TEN DOLLARS REWARD.

RAN AWAY from the subscriber, a *Negro man* named *Charles*, and a *Negro woman* named *Dorcas*. The man is about forty years old, and the woman thirty-eight. The man is very black—about five feet nine inches in height,—with the African marks on his face of his native country. The woman is about five feet nine inches, and rather thick set. Any person returning them shall receive the above reward. **HENRY W. MAXEY.**

Cedar Point, March 4.   1w10

Advertisement for runaway slave.
Jacksonville Courier

SOUTH FLORIDA TOOK MANY YEARS to develop and attract settlers. That was because the Native Americans there during the 19th century sometimes attacked settlers; also the mosquitoes and heat made life very hard 100 years ago. Little by little, settlers, including African Americans, made their way to the area to begin new careers and see what the land offered them.

One such African American was Henry, a man whose last name we do not know. He was a man who showed great courage in his job. He worked at **Cape Florida Light-** house, a tall brick tower at the southern tip of **Key Biscayne** east of Miami. For over 150 years, that lighthouse has warned ships about the reef that lies offshore and has guided boat captains through the waters there. Something happened in 1836 that almost destroyed the lighthouse.

When the **Second Seminole War** started in 1835, many people living in Miami left the area; many went to **Key West** or northern cities. Henry remained at the lighthouse to help the man taking care of the lighthouse, John Thompson. On July 23, 1836, Native Americans attacked the lighthouse, hoping to capture Henry and Thompson. The two men heard the Native Ameri-

DISCUSSION TOPICS: As you read this chapter, think about the answers to these questions: 1. Why do you think the Native Americans attacked the white settlers in south Florida? 2. Can you think of any methods used today to rescue people who are high above the ground in a building or on a bridge with no easy way to get down? 3. What would you have done in Thompson's place if you found yourself at the top of a lighthouse that Native Americans were attacking?

VOCABULARY
Cape Florida Lighthouse, Key Biscayne,
Second Seminole War, Key West,
gunpowder

Cape Florida Lighthouse
Florida State Archives

cans, realized the danger they were in, and ran to the lighthouse. They got inside the tower and locked the door just as the Native Americans raced toward them. The Native Americans were firing their guns.

Thompson stood by the window and fired his gun at the Native Americans to keep them away from the one door into the lighthouse. When night came, it became very dark; that made it difficult for Thompson to see the Native Americans. The Native Americans then sneaked up to the door and set it on fire. Thompson and the faithful Henry took a barrel of **gunpowder**, some bullets, and a gun and began climbing the steep ladder to the top of the tower. As Thompson and Henry climbed up, they cut off the ladder below them so that the Native Americans could not climb up after them.

When the fire had burned down the door, the Native Americans went into the lighthouse. Then they began shooting their guns up the tower to try to hit Thompson and Henry. One of the bullets wounded Henry, and he soon died. He had refused to leave Thompson, but instead met his death as bravely as he could.

When Thompson realized that the Native Americans had killed Henry, he thought that he would probably die soon also. He lifted up the barrel of gunpowder and threw it down the lighthouse tower. He wanted to blow up the whole building, even if that would mean he would also die. When the gunpowder exploded, however, the tower remained standing. The explosion was so loud that a U.S. ship 12 miles away heard it and came to Thompson's rescue.

The story of Henry at Cape Florida Lighthouse was like that of many African Americans in south Florida. They were brave and loyal to their friends and fellow workers.

Bill Baggs Cape Florida State Park and The Cape Florida Lighthouse
Location: 1200 South Crandon Boulevard, Key Biscayne
    Hours: Daily 8 - sunset.
Fees: $3.25 per vehicle, maximum of 8 people per car.

Further reading:
Kevin M. McCarthy, "Cape Florida Lighthouse," in *Florida Lighthouses* (Gainesville: University of Florida Press, 1990), pp. 41-44.

7.
BLACK SEMINOLES, 1838

IN THE 16TH AND 17TH CENTURIES there were not many people living in Florida. The land seemed difficult to farm, the mosquitoes and flies were awful, and they kept settlers away. Because Florida did not have many people, it seemed to be a good place for runaway slaves to escape from plantations in Georgia and South Carolina.

They joined another group of runaways: Native Americans who were escaping the Creek Native Americans and heading to Florida to begin a new life; these Native Americans called themselves **"Seminoles,"** which meant "runaways." The slaves and Seminoles joined forces, and a new people was born: the Black Seminoles.

In the early 1700s there were more than 100,000 such Black Seminoles. The white plantation owners in Florida did not like to see the joining of the runaway slaves and the Native Americans because that might encourage more slaves to escape from their owners. The African Americans turned out to be good friends of the Seminoles because the former slaves knew the weaknesses of the whites who had once kept them as slaves. They also acted as **interpreters**

Ben Bruno, an African American interpreter and assistant to Chief Billy Bowlegs.

Florida State Archives

DISCUSSION TOPICS: As you read this chapter, think about the answers to these questions: 1. Why do you think the runaway slaves and the Seminoles got along so well? 2. What words would you want placed on your gravestone? 3. What methods do you think slave catchers used to capture runaway slaves?

VOCABULARY
Seminoles, interpreters, scouts, Medal of Honor, gravestones

between the whites and the Native Americans. One interpreter was Abraham, sometimes called Negro Abraham.

Many times the African Americans married Seminoles and raised their children together. In 1818, General Andrew Jackson entered Florida to attack the Seminoles. That action pushed the Native Americans and their African American friends further south and east. Jackson's action also led to Florida being taken over from Spain by the United States in 1821. After that many Americans entered Florida to settle down and raise their families. The Seminoles and the African Americans fought many battles with the new

settlers and the army sent by officials in Washington, D.C.

When the U.S. Army entered Florida to destroy the Seminole villages and help more white settlers move in, the Second Seminole War began. It continued from 1835 until 1842. The soldiers wanted to defeat the

Abraham, an African American slave of Chief Micanopy
Florida State Archives

Seminoles and return the African American runaway slaves to their former owners.

When Andrew Jackson was president of the United States, he wanted the Seminoles in Florida to move west to places like Oklahoma. Abraham, the African American interpreter, went with a group of Seminole chiefs to inspect the land west of the Mississippi River that the U.S. government wanted the Native Americans to move to. Nearly 500 African Americans joined their friends, the Seminoles, in the long trip to Oklahoma between 1838 and 1843. They would never see Florida again.

Once there, the Black Seminoles continued to be troubled by slave catchers, men who wanted to catch the African Americans and make them slaves. About 300 Black

Gopher John, an African American Seminole interpreter for U.S. troops who were fighting the Seminoles.
Florida State Archives

Seminoles left Oklahoma and went to Mexico, where they worked as **scouts** and as patrols along the border between Mexico and the U.S.

After the Civil War ended in 1865, many of those Black Seminoles returned to the United States. There they worked as scouts for the U.S. Army until 1914. From 1873 to 1881 those Black Seminole scouts fought hostile Native Americans in 25 battles, but not a single man of their unit was killed or seriously wounded, and four of them received the **Medal of Honor** for bravery.

One of those who received the Medal of Honor was Adam Paine. Although little is known of his life, he seems to have been one of those who joined the Seminoles when they went west from Florida. In a battle with the Comanche Native Americans in Texas,

Adam Paine showed his courage. On September 20, 1874, a huge band of Native Americans attacked Paine and his group of soldiers. His commander later mentioned how brave Paine was in fighting off the Native Americans. Paine was the first Florida-born Black Seminole to win the very important Medal of Honor from the U.S. government.

Today in southwestern Texas near the Mexican border one can see **gravestones** of Seminoles that say "Born in Florida."

Further reading:
Daniel F. Littlefield, Jr., *Africans and Seminoles* (Westport, CT: Greenwood Press, 1977); Kenneth W. Porter, *The Negro on the American Frontier* (New York: Arno Press and the *New York Times*, 1971); Scott Thybony, "Against All Odds, Black Seminoles Won Their Freedom," *Smithsonian* (August 1991), pp. 90-101.

8.

THE ABOLITIONISTS, 1844

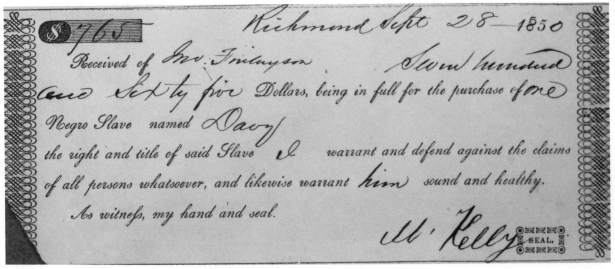

The receipt for a slave purchased in Richmond, VA, for a man in Jefferson County, FL, in 1850

Florida State Archives

ABOLITIONISTS WERE PEOPLE WHO wanted to get rid of slavery in the United States. From around 1835 until the end of the Civil War in 1865, they established newspapers and did their best to try to get rid of slavery as quickly as possible in this country. The **Underground Railroad** was set up by abolitionists as a way to help slaves escape to Canada and the free states of the North.

One abolitionist was Jonathan Walker, a white man from Massachusetts who had had many troubles growing up. Those troubles made him put a high value on life. When he was 15, he fell through an ice pond and

nearly drowned. After he became a sailor, he was knocked out on a ship during a terrible storm. A year later (1820), he fell from a ship into the sea on a dark night and almost drowned. In 1824 he was in Havana, Cuba, during a yellow fever **epidemic**, but survived. When he was in Mexico, robbers attacked him and shot at him, but he managed to escape by swimming away in the darkness. All of these experiences made him stronger and made him value life, especially a free life, including that of slaves.

While he was living in Pensacola, Florida, Walker came to understand how hard a life the slaves had there and in the rest of the South. He once saw a slave cut off his own thumb and index finger with an axe in order to make himself less valuable in the

DISCUSSION TOPICS: As you read this chapter, think about the answers to these questions: 1. If you had been alive in the 19th century in the United States and believed that slavery was wrong, how would you go about trying to end it? 2. If Jonathan Walker broke the law by trying to help some slaves escape, how do you think he should have been punished? 3. If you were a local sheriff in Pensacola in 1844, how would you have treated Jonathan Walker?

VOCABULARY
abolitionists, Underground Railroad,
epidemic, brand

25

slave market. He learned that some local men used vicious dogs and guns to hunt down and torture escaping slaves. These and other experiences made him decide in 1844 to help some local slaves escape in his small boat to Nassau, a city on a British island off the east coast of Florida where the slaves could find freedom.

After Walker and his escaping slaves had been at sea for 14 days and had traveled 700 miles, a passing ship came upon them. The crew and captain of the ship discovered what Walker was trying to do. The captain then arrested him for helping the slaves escape from the United States. Officers took Walker back to Pensacola. There he was found guilty and punished by having the letters "SS" for "slave stealer" burned into his right palm. The man in charge of burning

Walker's palm held the hot **brand** on Walker's hand for 15 seconds.

After Walker was released from jail in 1845, he returned to his home in New England. A New England poet, John Greenleaf Whittier, wrote a well-known poem, "The Branded Hand," about what had happened to the abolitionist. Part of that poem had lines that praised Walker:

> Welcome home again, brave seaman!
>   with thy thoughtful brow and gray,
> And the old heroic spirit of our earlier,
>   better day;
> With that front of calm endurance, on
>   whose steady nerve in vain
> Pressed the iron of the prison, smote the
>   fiery shafts of pain!
> Then lift that manly right-hand, bold
>   ploughman of the waves!
> Its branded palm shall prophesy, "Sal-
>   vation to the Slave!"
> Hold up its fire-wrought language, that
>   whoso reads may feel
> His heart swell strong within him, his
>   sinews change to steel.

Before he died in 1878, Walker wrote a small book, *The Branded Hand*, about his experiences. His book made many people in the North angry about slavery. They wanted to do all they could to fight slavery. Although Walker and many others worked hard for the abolition of slavery, it would still take a lot of time and a Civil War to do it. It was not until 1868 that the addition of the Fourteenth Amendment to the U.S. Constitution granted citizenship and equal rights to African Americans. Even then, it would take many more years of struggle for African Americans in this country to begin to gain their rights.

Further reading:
Jonathan Walker, *The Branded Hand: Trial and Imprisonment of Jonathan Walker* (New York: Arno Press, 1969).

Charity Stewart, Former Slave, Age 93
Florida State Archives

9.

FLORIDA THE SLAVE STATE, 1845

Picking cotton in north Florida
Florida State Archives

FROM THE TIME the United States took control of Florida from the Spanish in 1821, people from other states began moving here to settle and farm the land. The **Seminole Wars** between the federal forces and the Native Americans discouraged some people from moving to Florida, but others came when the federal government offered them free land in 1842. The population of the Florida territory then was as follows:

Year	Total Population	White	Nonwhite Slave	Free	Nonwhite as a percentage of total population
1830	34,730	18,385	15,501	844	47%
1840	54,477	27,943	25,717	817	48%
1850	87,445	47,203	39,310	932	46%
1860	140,424	77,746	61,746	932	45%

DISCUSSION TOPICS: As you read this chapter, think about the answers to these questions: 1. If you had been a slave, do you think you would have (a) tried to escape, (b) learned a skill that would have taken you out of the cotton fields, (c) done whatever the plantation owner wanted you to do, or (d) what? 2. Was it worth it for slaves to try to escape by boat to freedom in the Bahamas? 3. What do you think bosses do today to their workers that reminds you of a kind of slavery?

VOCABULARY
Seminole Wars, economy, secede, Gulf Stream, waterspout, mast

The nonwhite population made up over 40% of the people of Florida. The majority of the nonwhite population were slaves; fewer than a thousand of the nonwhite population were free. The free African Americans lived in places like Pensacola, Jacksonville, and Key West and worked as sailors, farmers, craftsmen, and laborers.

Many people living in Florida wanted the territory to become a state. If it did become a state, its citizens could vote for its officials instead of having them appointed by the president of the United States. Because Florida depended on slave labor to work on its farms, it would be a slave state if it entered the Union. But the U.S. Congress would not admit it unless another territory entered the Union at the same time as a free state. In that way Congress could keep the balance between free and slave states. Finally in 1845, Iowa entered the Union as a free state, and Florida entered as a slave state.

The life of the slave was very difficult. In a work called *American Slavery As It Is: Testimony of a Thousand Witnesses* (New York: American Anti-Slavery Society, 1839, p. 38) one visitor to Florida described slavery in Florida as follows:

> It is not uncommon for hands, in hurrying times, beside working all day, to labor half the night. This is usually the case on sugar plantations, during the sugar-boiling season; and on cotton, during its gathering. Beside the regular task of picking cotton, averaging of the short staple, when the crop is good, 100 pounds a day to the hand, the ginning (extracting the seed), and baling was done in the night. Said Mr. – to me, while conversing upon the customary labor slaves, "I work my niggers in a hurrying time till 11 or 12 o'clock at night, and have them up by four in the morning."

Florida's **economy** continued to depend on the hard labor of its many slaves. In the next 15 years, from 1845 until 1860, Americans throughout the country would argue a lot for or against slavery. At the end of those 15 years Florida would vote to leave the Union, to **secede**, and to join other Southern states in the Civil War. One slave working in Florida was Mauma (see photo on page 29), a woman who was brought to South Carolina from Africa on a slave ship. In the 1830s she was brought to Florida and worked for a family in Jefferson County. One of the people in that family wrote the following about her in 1873:

> We buried either in [18]57 or [18]58 our faithful old "Mauma" Mollie – her who had nursed nearly all of the children of the family; been a friend as well as faithful servant to my Mother; in whose cabin we had often eaten the homely meal of fried bacon and ash cake and where we always had welcome and sympathy and whom we loved as a second mother. Black of skin but pure of heart, she doubtless stands among the faithful on the right of the King.

Runaway slaves sometimes headed south to reach present-day Dade County. There they could escape across the **Gulf Stream**, which flows off the east coast of Florida, to freedom in the Bahamas. The painting on the cover of this book represents one such person who might have been trying to get away from his slave owners in north Florida. The painting, done by an artist called Winslow Homer, is called "The Gulf Stream."

If you look carefully at the picture, you can see that the man in the boat has a lot of problems. A ship in the upper left-hand part of the painting might have been out looking for escaping slaves in order to capture them and return them to their owners. The **waterspout** in the upper right-hand part of the painting could sink the man's little boat if it

Mauma, a slave in Jefferson County
Florida State Archives

came his way. The sharks in the water are swimming near the boat in hopes of having him for dinner. The **mast** on the boat is broken; that makes it impossible to sail; the boat has to go wherever the wind and ocean take it. The man seems to have no water or food. We chose this picture for the front of this book because it represents the bad situation of the African American in Florida in the 19th century. African Americans suffered much in this state, and some still continue to suffer.

Further reading:

John W. Blassingame, editor, *Slave Testimony: Two Centuries of Letters, Speeches, Interviews, and Autobiographies* (Baton Rouge, LA: Louisiana State University Press, 1977); Gary R. Mormino, "Florida Slave Narratives," *Florida Historical Quarterly* (April 1988), pp. 399-419; George P. Rawick, editor, *The American Slave: A Composite Autobiography*, Vol. 17: *Florida Narratives* (Westport, CT: Greenwood Publishing Company, 1941); Julia Floyd Smith, *Slavery and Plantation Growth in Antebellum Florida, 1821-1860* (Gainesville, FL: University of Florida Press, 1973).

10.

THE CIVIL WAR, 1861-1865

THE 1850s WERE A DIFFICULT TIME for the United States. People in the North and people in the South argued a lot about the good points and bad points of slavery. Many Florida farmers who had slaves thought that slavery was necessary in order to produce the crops that the Florida economy depended on, especially cotton. They also thought they treated their slaves well. They could not see how making slaves of fellow human beings was wrong. They disagreed with those Americans who said that our Declaration of Independence, which stated that "all men are created equal," applied to slaves.

The publication of *Uncle Tom's Cabin* by **Harriet Beecher Stowe** in 1852 showed many people the evils of slavery. In the novel, Simon Legree, a cruel owner of slaves, hurts them without any mercy. A Florida writer, Caroline Hentz, wrote a novel, *Planter's Northern Bride*, to try to point out the good points of slavery, but the book was not as

The escaped slave in the Union Army
Library of Congress

DISCUSSION TOPICS: As you read this chapter, think about the answers to these questions: 1. Do you think that Florida is still a good place to raise cattle and hogs? Where do you think ranchers raise cattle and hogs in Florida? 2. Why do you think that, when the Civil War finally ended in 1865, many freed slaves remained in Florida rather than go north to look for work? 3. What do you think changed in Florida after the Civil War that attracted so many people to visit and stay?

VOCABULARY
Harriet Beecher Stowe, outlaw,
Confederate, Union

Fort Clinch in Fernandina
Kevin M. McCarthy

popular as *Uncle Tom's Cabin*. Abolitionists wanted our country to **outlaw** slavery throughout the United States. Years later Harriet Beecher Stowe would move to Florida with her husband, but by that time many Floridians were no longer angry at her for writing about slavery. (See below, Chapter 14.)

As the important national election of 1860 grew closer, people in Florida and other southern states grew nervous over the possible election of Abraham Lincoln. Florida still did not have many people — only about 140,000. A little less than half of that number were African Americans.

The most important cities in the state were St. Augustine in the east and Pensacola in the west. In between lay many plantations where slaves worked the cotton fields and did their best just to stay alive. When Lincoln

was elected president in November 1860, the southern or **Confederate** states, including Florida, decided to leave the Union, to secede.

During the Civil War, which began in 1861, very few battles were fought in Florida. That was because Florida was so far away from Virginia and other states more directly involved in the war. Also Florida sent most of its soldiers north to fight battles there. What Florida did supply to the other Confederate states was cattle and hogs; the state had some 660,000 head of cattle and thousands of hogs, and many of them were shipped to other southern states to help feed the troops.

Some Florida cities like Key West remained in **Union** hands during the war. Key West became a place where federal ships could take slaves they had rescued from slave ships. Other cities, like Jacksonville,

31

were controlled, first by one side and then by the other at different times during the war.

In 1863, a troop of 1,400 African Americans from the Union side sailed up the St. Johns River, trying to get slaves along the way to join them. Making such a trip was very dangerous for the African American soldiers because, if Confederate troops captured them, those troops might treat the African Americans very badly. Many other slaves remained loyal to their masters and continued working on the plantations and farms during the war.

When the war finally ended in 1865 and the slaves were freed, many of them remained in Florida rather than go north to look for work. Other freed slaves went north in hopes of beginning a new life. It would take a lot more work and a lot more suffering before the freed slaves began to see success, but they were hopeful all would turn out well.

Further reading:

William Watson Davis, *Civil War and Reconstruction in Florida* (Gainesville: University of Florida Press, 1964).

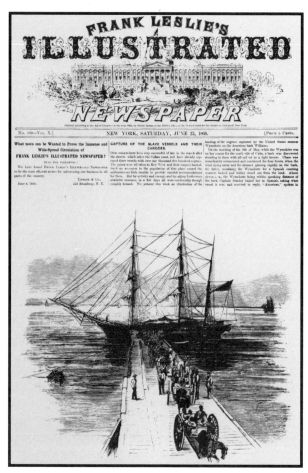

A captured cargo of slaves being unloaded in Key West in 1860
Frank Leslie's Illustrated Newspaper

11.
THE BATTLE OF OLUSTEE, 1864

Battle of Olustee
Florida State Archives

THE MOST IMPORTANT **land battle** fought in Florida during the Civil War was the Battle of Olustee in February 1864. Union troops heading west from Jacksonville met a large Confederate force at a place called Ocean Pond near Lake City. There, on February 20, the troops on each side fought in what came to be known as the Battle of Olustee. The two forces that faced each other were about equal in number; each had between 5,000 and 5,500 soldiers.

What the Union side had that the Confederate did not have were African American troops. Those soldiers on the Union side included the 8th U.S. Colored, the First North Carolina, and the 54th Massachusetts. One of the soldiers in the 54th Massachusetts was Sergeant William H. Carney, who was the first African American to win the Medal of

DISCUSSION TOPICS: As you read this chapter, think about the answers to these questions: 1. Why do you think the Union side in the American Civil War had African American troops, but the Confederate side did not? 2. Why do generals and other commanders sometimes order their troops to retreat in a battle? 3. If you were in charge of a museum at a place like the Battle of Olustee, what would you put in the museum for visitors to see?

> *VOCABULARY*
> land battle, battlefield, prisons, retreat

Honor; we mentioned this medal above in the chapter on Black Seminoles, 1838. He was honored for his bravery in leading the other soldiers at the Battle of Fort Wagner, South Carolina, even though he had been wounded twice.

The African Americans who fought for the Union side at the Battle of Olustee knew they faced a very difficult situation. If they were wounded and left behind on the **battlefield,** the Southern soldiers might kill them or injure them or send them to terrible **prisons** such as the one at Andersonville in Georgia. The fighting was very hard. Many men died or fell wounded as the battle continued. As the Confederates began to win the battle, the Union commanders ordered their soldiers to **retreat.** The 54th Massachusetts did particularly well as it fired its guns, fell back 100 yards, and fired again.

The Confederates won the six-hour battle and forced the Union troops back toward Jacksonville. After marching all night, the Union commander ordered the African Americans back toward the battle place to help wounded soldiers on a train stuck on the railroad tracks. The idea of going back toward the Confederate troops was difficult, but the African Americans did it in order to save the wounded soldiers on the train. When they reached the stuck train, they used ropes to pull the train down the tracks for several miles. When they finally helped the train continue on its way, they marched to Jacksonville. Those African Americans were very brave and helped save other soldiers who were wounded in the battle.

The doctor who served with the 8th U.S. Colored Troops later described the great courage of those troops:

Here they stood for two hours and a half, under one of the most terrible fires I ever witnessed; and here, on the field of Olustee, was decided whether the colored man had the

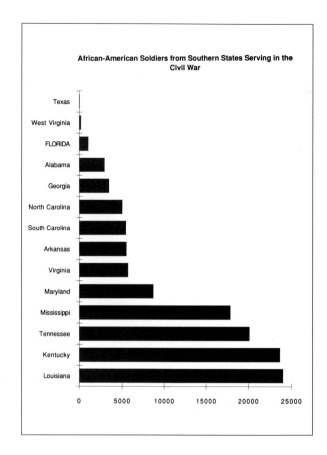

courage to stand without shelter, and risk the dangers of the battlefield; and when I tell you that they stood with a fire in front, on their flank, and in their rear, for two hours and a half, without flinching, and when I tell you the number of dead and wounded, I have no doubt as to the verdict of every man who has gratitude for the defenders of his country, white or black.

Olustee Battlefield

Location: 2.5 miles east of Olustee on U.S. 90
Hours: Battlefield: daily 8-5;
          Museum: Thursday - Monday 8 - 5
Fees: No charge
Phone: (904) 752-3866
Reenactment of battle: Each year men dressed in the military uniforms of both sides show visitors how the battle was fought.

12.
RECONSTRUCTION, 1865-1877

Selling a freedman to pay his fine
Florida State Archives

AS THE CIVIL WAR ENDED, Florida had some very serious problems. As those Florida soldiers who had served in the Confederate army came home, they found that much had changed since they had left. The slaves were free. Union soldiers were in charge of the state. Most people had little or no money and therefore could not plant their crops.

DISCUSSION TOPICS: As you read this chapter, think about the answers to these questions: 1. If you were a Confederate soldier returning to your home after the American Civil War, what steps would you take to get your house and lands back in shape? 2. How do you think life changed on Southern plantations after the American Civil War? 3. Describe the scene of the African American casting his first vote, as pictured in the sketch on page 36.

Many freed slaves remained in Florida to help their former owners plant crops and run farms. But now the slaves were paid in money or crops. Some of the **freedmen**, who used to be slaves, rented out land from former slave owners. The Freedmen's Bureau helped many former slaves work on their former farms for money, but the amount of money they earned was so small that many African Americans found themselves in a

> *VOCABULARY*
> freedmen, turpentine camps, lynch,
> Reconstruction, carpetbaggers,
> constitutional convention,
> act of secession, Black Codes

type of slavery on the farms and in the **turpentine camps.** (For more about turpentine camps see Chapter 20.)

Many white Floridians were afraid that African Americans would be running the state of Florida; some left for places like South America instead of staying in Florida. Others joined the Ku Klux Klan and looked at night for African Americans to hurt, even to **lynch.**

Voting for the first time
Harper's Weekly

The time after the Civil War became known as **Reconstruction,** a time when the nation tried to come back together again. Reconstruction lasted in Florida from 1865, when the Civil War ended, until 1877, when federal troops left the state. Many people from the North came to Southern states like Florida with different ideas about how to treat southerners. Some northerners wanted to punish Southerners for fighting the Civil War. Others, called **"carpetbaggers"** because they seemed to carry all of their clothes and articles in one piece of luggage (a carpetbag), came south looking for ways to make money. Others were concerned about

the poor schools or lack of schools and wanted to educate Southerners, white and African American.

At the end of the war, in December 1865, Florida had a **constitutional convention** that repealed (did away with) the **act of secession** and slavery. The Florida Legislature passed laws, called **"Black Codes,"** that tried to keep the former slaves down and in a new kind of slavery. Those Black Codes said that the state could put to death an African American who raped a white woman or who encouraged others in rebellion. The Codes also did not allow African Americans to own guns, knives, or any other weapon. Those Codes allowed the police to arrest African Americans and sentence them to forced labor for up to a year.

Such Black Codes so angered the U.S. Congress that it put Southern states under military rule. During Reconstruction African Americans in Florida ran for public office and won. They served in local governments and also in the state legislature in Tallahassee. The Ku Klux Klan remained active in the state and tried to keep African Americans from voting or holding political office. In fact, it would take another hundred years before African Americans began to have the equal rights they should have had.

Further reading:
Joe M. Richardson, *The Negro in the Reconstruction of Florida, 1865-1877* (Tallahassee: The Florida State University, 1965); Jerrell H. Shofner, *Nor Is It Over Yet: Florida During the Era of Reconstruction, 1863-1877* (Gainesville: University of Florida Press, 1974); Theodore Brantner Wilson, *The Black Codes of the South* (University, AL: University of Alabama Press, 1965).

13.
ROBERT MEACHAM, 1835-1902

Robert Meacham

ONE OF THE GREAT AFRICAN AMERICAN leaders in Florida during Reconstruction was Robert Meacham. He helped establish the African Methodist Episcopal Church in Florida. In the **Florida Legislature** he helped establish the state's public education system. And he served as postmaster in Punta Gorda, Florida.

His mother was a slave, and his father was a white doctor who taught young Robert how to read and write. When asked if he was born a slave or a free person, Robert answered, "I do not know how to answer that exactly, for my father was my master and always told me that I was free." When Robert began attending a white school in Quincy, Florida, the parents of the white students objected, and so Robert had to stop attending that school.

DISCUSSION TOPICS: As you read this chapter, think about the answers to these questions: 1. How do you think public schools differ from private schools? 2. Today Meacham Early Childhood Center in Tampa honors Robert Meacham's daughter-in-law; can you think of any other buildings in your town or city that honor people? 3. If you were the superintendent of schools in your county, what would you change?

> *VOCABULARY*
> Florida Legislature, pastor, constitution, superintendent of schools, postmaster, daughter-in-law, father-in-law

Stella   Christina Meacham

When Robert was working as a servant in Tallahassee, he met his future wife, Stella, another servant. Robert worked hard and was able to buy his freedom and his mother's freedom from slavery. After the Civil War ended in 1865, Robert became a **pastor** of the African Methodist Church (A.M.E.) in Tallahassee. He later moved to Monticello, Florida, to work in a church and Jefferson County's first school for freed slaves.

In 1868, he became a member of a group of people that wrote a new **constitution** for Florida. He worked very hard to have the constitution mention that everyone in Florida had the right to a free public education. He became **superintendent of schools** and **postmaster** in Monticello and worked to help everyone in the city. But not everyone liked him; one night in 1876 two white men shot at him with their pistols, but he escaped.

In 1889, Robert became postmaster in Punta Gorda, Florida, a small town on the west coast of Florida. He later moved to

Tampa, where he ran a shoe shop and where he died on February 27, 1902. He had served Florida well and did much to encourage everyone, white and African American, to attend school and get the best education they could.

His **daughter-in-law**, Christina Meacham, became the first African American woman principal of a Tampa school. Ms. Meacham (1865-1927) taught for 40 years. Today Meacham Early Childhood Center in Tampa honors this great educator. Thousands of children in Tampa owe much of their education to Ms. Meacham, a woman who followed the example set by her **father-in-law**, Robert Meacham.

Further reading:

Canter Brown, Jr., "'Where Are Now the Hopes I Cherished?' The Life and Times of Robert Meacham." *The Florida Historical Quarterly* Vol. 69 (July 1990) pp. 1-36.

14.
HARRIET BEECHER STOWE, 1867

Harriet Beecher Stowe
Dictionary of American Portraits

ONE WOMAN WHO SPENT MUCH OF HER LIFE in the North and in Florida working to help African Americans was Harriet Beecher Stowe (1811-1896). She is most famous for writing *Uncle Tom's Cabin* (1852), the story of **slavery** in the South. This book was published nine years before the beginning of the Civil War and made readers throughout America and the world realize just how terrible the condition of slavery was in the South.

Two years after the Civil War ended in 1865, she rented a cotton plantation in Florida. She wanted to give freed slaves the opportunity to earn money and thus help themselves and their families. She wanted her son, who had been wounded in the Civil War, to run the plantation and get his health back. After she lost $10,000 in the project, she gave it up.

DISCUSSION TOPICS: As you read this chapter, think about the answers to these questions: 1. If you had lived at the time of the Civil War and had a lot of money, how could you have spent that money to help the ex-slaves? 2. If you had two friends who disagreed about an issue like slavery, how would you try to get them to sit down and talk about it without fighting? 3. If you were writing about the good parts of Florida, as Harriet Beecher Stowe did, what would you mention? What are the bad parts about living in this state? Can you write two paragraphs about one place in Florida, one paragraph pointing out the good parts of that place and one paragraph about the bad parts of that same place?

> *VOCABULARY*
> slavery, steamboats, memorial

Man & woman posed as if pulling and pushing a plow
Florida State Archives

But she discovered how pleasant it was to live in Florida in the winter because of the mild climate here. She was from New England, where ice and snow make winters difficult.

She and her family bought some property in the small town of Mandarin, which is on the St. Johns River near Jacksonville. There they would spend the winter reading, writing, and boating on the river. People traveling up the St. Johns River on **steamboats** sometimes caught sight of Mrs. Stowe and her family sitting on the porch of their home reading and talking.

Mrs. Stowe began writing about Florida's sunshine, flowers, and orange crops. These writings were later published in a book called *Palmetto-Leaves* (1873). That book was so popular among readers in the North that many tourists began coming to Florida – and still come today. In that book she praised

the African Americans who worked for her as hard workers and honest neighbors. She especially liked the children: "The negro children are bright; they can be taught any thing."

Mrs. Stowe was also greatly interested in the education of the African American children in Mandarin. She taught Sunday school and helped establish a school for the children there; its first teacher was a woman from Brooklyn, New York. Mrs. Stowe used to hand out spelling books, which the children would eagerly read. They would show up after work and on Sundays asking her to teach them as much as possible.

In 1874, after her brother was put in charge of education in Florida, she visited him in Tallahassee. There the local people turned out to honor her and shake her hand. She stood on the steps of a public building and shook hands with dozens of people.

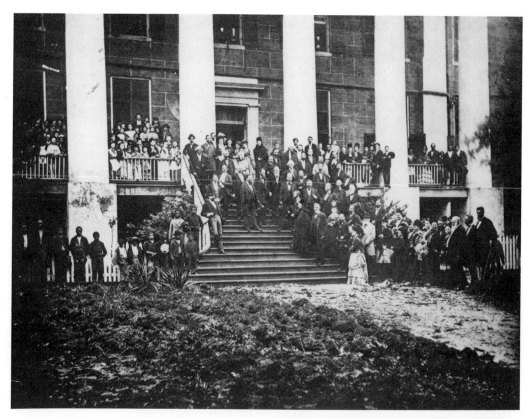

Harriet Beecher Stowe visiting Tallahassee
Florida State Archives

Today, if you visit Mandarin, Florida, you can see a sign about Harriet Beecher Stowe in the community building. The west window of the Episcopal Church of Our Savior there is a **memorial** to the Stowe family.

Further reading:
John R. Adams, *Harriet Beecher Stowe* (Boston: Twayne Publishers, 1989); Mary B. Graff, *Mandarin on the St. Johns* (Gainesville: University of Florida Press, 1953); Harriet Beecher Stowe, *Palmetto-Leaves* (Gainesville: University of Florida Press, 1968)

15.
JOSIAH WALLS, 1842-1905

Josiah Walls
Florida State Archives

JOSIAH WALLS WAS BORN IN VIRGINIA in 1842 and later worked as a **miller**. In 1863, two years after the Civil War began, he became a member of an African American troop and fought for the Union side, the North. After fighting in several battles and being promoted to sergeant, he was sent to Jacksonville as an **artillery instructor**.

When the war ended, he decided to stay in Florida and settled near Alachua. He needed to find work to support himself and his new bride, and so he got a job cutting down trees and floating the logs to lumber camps. After leaving that job, Walls became a school teacher in Archer. As more and more African Americans registered to vote, they realized they needed someone who could

---

DISCUSSION TOPICS: As you read this chapter, think about the answers to these questions: 1. How do you think the jobs of lumberer and teacher helped Josiah Walls be a good Congressman? 2. If you were going to start a newspaper in your school or town, what would you call it? Why? 3. Discuss the job of trash collector as pictured in the photo. Compare that position with one of trash collector today.

> *VOCABULARY*
> miller, artillery instructor, delegate, House of Representatives, mayor, Congressman, customhouses

Trash collector
Florida State Archives

speak for their side. They found such a spokesman in Josiah Walls and, in 1867, sent him to Tallahassee as a **delegate** to the state Republican Convention.

The following year he was elected to the state **House of Representatives**. In 1869, he was elected to the state Senate. The following summer he was nominated to run for United States Congressman. He won the election and went to Washington. Walls was reelected in 1872 and again in 1874 before finally being defeated in 1876.

In 1873, Walls bought a newspaper in Gainesville called the *New Era*; that paper was the first Florida newspaper owned by an African American. He promised that the "wants and interests of the people of color will receive special attention." He also served as **mayor** of Gainesville, which shows how busy he was and how hard he worked.

For several years he was Florida's only **Congressman** in the House of Representatives in Washington. He would be the last African American representing Florida until the November 1992 election that sent Corrine Brown, Alcee Hastings, and Carrie Meek to represent the state in Washington.

Josiah Walls contributed to a number of very important improvements in the state, for example, the grant of 90,000 acres of land to the people in charge of the Florida Agricultural College. Many **customhouses**, post offices, and other federal buildings were built in the state during the time he was in office, and mail service was greatly improved. When he left politics, he returned to farming and was in charge of the farm at the State College at Tallahassee when he died on May 15, 1905. He was buried in the Negro Cemetery in Tallahassee.

Further reading:
Peter D. Klingman, *Josiah Walls* (Gainesville: University Presses of Florida, 1976). Also "Josiah T. Walls/Florida" in *Black Americans in Congress* by Maurine Christopher (New York: Thomas Y. Crowell Company, 1976), pp. 78-86.

16.
JONATHAN C. GIBBS, 1827-1874

Jonathan C. Gibbs
Florida State Archives

DISCUSSION TOPICS: As you read this chapter, think about the answers to these questions: 1. Do you think we should first teach people how to read and write or should we teach them how to get a job that pays them money? 2. What would you want named after you to honor you some day? 3. If you thought a hate group like the Ku Klux Klan was after you, how would you protect yourself or live your life differently?

JONATHAN C. GIBBS, who was born in Philadelphia, Pennsylvania, in 1827 of free parents, was the son of a Methodist minister. After his father died, Jonathan worked as a carpenter, but later became a minister in the Presbyterian Church. He earned a degree at Dartmouth College and also studied at Princeton Theological Seminary. After the Civil War ended in 1865, he traveled to North Carolina, where he opened a school for the freed slaves. In 1867, he went south to Florida to work with the newly freed slaves there.

After Harrison Reed was elected governor of Florida in 1868, Reed appointed Gibbs his **secretary of state**. Gibbs served in that position from 1869 until 1872 and was the only African American in the **cabinet** at that time. The next Florida governor, Ossian Hart, appointed Gibbs **state superintendent of public instruction** in charge of Florida's schools. At that time more than one-third of the state's 200,000 people could not read or write. Many of those **illiterate** people were African Americans who had worked on plantations. They had wanted to learn to read and write but had not had any chance to do so. Gibbs made the school system better, adopted standard textbooks, and established many schools for African Americans. Within a year or so he had done so well in encouraging African Americans to attend school that al-

> *VOCABULARY*
> secretary of state, cabinet,
> state superintendent of public instruction,
> illiterate, Union Academy, historians

Union Academy in Gainesville

most one-third of the students were African Americans. All students gained a lot from the textbooks that Gibbs helped provide the schools.

Typical of the schools set up in Florida after the Civil War was the **Union Academy** in Gainesville. The Freedmen's Bureau established the school in 1866, but local whites did not like the school and did not support it. The school had to depend on hiring teachers from the North and on receiving financial help from people in the North in order to keep on educating the children of the recently freed slaves. The school began with elementary classes and later added a high school.

Jonathan Gibbs worked hard to help African Americans receive an education in Florida. He knew that his efforts angered many whites, and therefore he was careful about his own safety. He lived in a beautiful house in Tallahassee, but chose to sleep in the attic of the house rather than one of the bedrooms. He told his brother that he did this because he was afraid of the Ku Klux Klan. He also kept weapons near his bed in order

to protect himself in case the Ku Klux Klan attacked him at night.

One day in 1874 Gibbs gave a long speech to a large group of people and afterward went home to have dinner and relax. For some unknown reason, he died soon after dinner. Some people believed that his enemies poisoned him, but no one could find any proof of that. Jonathan Gibbs is today honored by having Gibbs High School in St. Petersburg named after him. Many **historians** believe that he did more for free public education in Florida than many other officials before or since. The city of Tallahassee named a street after him, Gibbs Drive.

Further reading:

Leedell W. Neyland, *Twelve Black Floridians* (Tallahassee, FL: Florida Agricultural and Mechanical University Foundation, 1970), pp. 1-5.

17.

EDWARD WATERS COLLEGE, 1872

MANY AFRICAN AMERICANS IN THE SOUTH knew that the more education they had, the better jobs they could obtain and the better they could help their families. Before the Civil War, African Americans, whether slave or free, had a difficult time finding a way to earn that education. White plantation owners did not want them to become educated. Sometimes the white slave owners would let some of their slaves learn to read so that the slaves could study the Bible and maybe teach the other slaves. But most slaves were not allowed to learn how to read or write.

After the Civil War more schools were opened up in the South for both whites and African Americans, often with the help of Union soldiers. Many times teachers came from the North to teach in these schools. Schools like Fisk University (1865), Atlanta University (1865), Howard University (1867),

Midwives attending a meeting at Edward Waters College in Jacksonville
Florida State Archives

DISCUSSION TOPICS: As you read this chapter, think about the answers to these questions: 1. Why is it so important to read and write in the world today?
2. What are the advantages and disadvantages of busing children across town to integrate schools?
3. How should the federal government fight the Ku Klux Klan?

A school for freedmen in the South in 1866
Florida State Archives

and Hampton Institute (1868) were established for African Americans. Such schools were often the target of attacks by the Ku Klux Klan and did not receive enough money to have good-looking buildings. But at least they were a start, and thousands of African Americans over the years learned a lot at the schools.

Edward Waters College in Jacksonville is the oldest independent institution of higher education in Florida. This four-year, **liberal arts** college that young men and women attend has close **ties** with the African Methodist Episcopal Church. It was the first such school established for the education of African Americans in Florida. Today approximately 670 students, most of whom are from north Florida and south Georgia, attend the college, which is situated on 20 acres in Jacksonville.

The history of the college began right after the end of the Civil War in 1865. That time, which is called the Reconstruction Period, saw four million African Americans, who had been slaves, struggling to do well in America. Very few slaves had learned to read and write, two necessary skills for success in the world. The African Methodist Episcopal Church wanted to start a school in Jacksonville for the African Americans in the area.

In 1872, the Florida Legislature established a school in Live Oak, Florida. Friends gave to the school 640 acres of land, a wagon, and two mules from the **state treasurer**. But nothing came of that first attempt, though; instead of paying the carpenters, the person in charge ran away with the money. He later drowned at sea.

Eleven years later, officials opened the school in Jacksonville. They later named it Edward Waters College after a bishop of the African Methodist Episcopal Church. A terrible fire in 1901 burned down the school, but three years later the college opened again.

Over the years the college has had a hard time raising money, as have many colleges in America. But it has survived and continues to serve many students in the Jacksonville area. Among the students who have gone to that school were A. Philip Randolph, founder of the Brotherhood of Sleeping Car Porters; and Dr. Andrew Robinson, dean of the College of Education at the University of North Florida.

Further reading:
Samuel J. Tucker, *Phoenix From the Ashes: EWC's Past, Present, and Future* (Jacksonville: Convention Press, 1976). For more about the school write: Edward Waters College, Jacksonville, FL 32209.

18.
T. THOMAS FORTUNE, 1856-1928

T. Thomas Fortune
Florida State Archives

ONE FLORIDA SLAVE who left the state and became a famous newspaper writer was Timothy Thomas Fortune. He was born in the small town of Marianna, Florida, on October 31, 1856. His **ancestors** included Seminole Native Americans and Irishmen. His father was a shoemaker and a **tanner**, that is, someone who made the skin of animals into leather.

Timothy used to spend Saturdays fishing in the nearby streams with his father. The fish they caught on Saturday made Sunday breakfasts that much better. Timothy also became quite good at shooting marbles and spent many an afternoon playing marbles with his friends. More important, he discovered two parts of Marianna that were to affect him the rest of his life: the school and the newspaper.

As the Civil War ended, two Union soldiers began gathering African Americans, adults as well as children, from Marianna into a small church. There the two soldiers taught everyone who came how to read and write. In that school young Timothy got "the book-learning fever" that stayed with him the rest of his life. He knew, even as a young man, how much he could do in life if he knew how to read well. White boys would sometimes

DISCUSSION TOPICS: As you read this chapter, think about the answers to these questions: 1. What do you think Timothy learned from fishing that he could use in other parts of his life? 2. What was the purpose of putting someone in the stocks for punishment, as pictured in the photograph? 3. How do you think a newspaper can influence the way people think?

VOCABULARY
ancestors, tanner, type,
Ku Klux Klan, congressman,

An African American receives a harsh punishment in Apalachicola   Florida State Archives

throw stones at the African American children going to school, but the children did not quit and became better and better at reading and writing.

Young Timothy also liked the local newspaper. One day he was walking by the place where workers produced the *Marianna Courier*. He went inside and found out how exciting newspaper work can be. He soon learned to set **type** for the weekly newspaper and learned as much of the newspaper business as he could. Working for newspapers would take him on to Jacksonville and New York City and make him one of the best-known writers of his day.

Timothy's father was elected to the Florida legislature, but later had to flee with his family to Jacksonville when the **Ku Klux Klan** began threatening African Americans. In Jacksonville young Timothy worked on a newspaper called the *Daily Union* and slowly became very good in writing and in learning how to publish a newspaper.

A **congressman** from Marianna, Florida, helped Timothy get a job in the state of Delaware, where Timothy saved enough money to attend Howard University. In 1881, Timothy Fortune, who had married his childhood sweetheart from Marianna, went to New York City to work on another newspaper, the *New York Globe*. That newspaper became one of the most important African American newspapers in the United States. Mr. Fortune became editor of that newspaper and one of the most important newspapermen in the country. He later worked for newspapers like the *Freeman*, the *New York Age*, and *The Negro World*. He established the National Afro-American League. He fought for equal rights for all African Americans.

When Mr. Fortune died in 1928 in Philadelphia, Pennsylvania, at the age of 71, he had spent his adult life fighting for the rights of African Americans throughout the United States, but especially in the South where he had grown up. He believed that the interests of African Americans and whites were "one and the same" and that human nature "is the same wherever mankind is found." He fought for full rights for all African Americans at a time when many people in this country did not agree with his ideas.

Fortune's life showed how far one can go with a good education, a strong religion, and a good family life. He was born a slave in a small Florida town, but studied hard and became one of the most important newspaper writers in the United States. He fought against the idea of "separate but equal" school systems and encouraged African Americans to do well in education.

Further reading:
Gene Burnett, "T.T. Fortune: Florida's Black Militant," in *Florida's Past: People and Events that Shaped the State*, Vol. I, pp. 50-53 (Sarasota: Pineapple Press, 1986). Emma Lou Thornbrough, *T. Thomas Fortune, Militant Journalist* (Chicago: University of Chicago Press, 1972).

19.

AFRICAN AMERICAN NEWSPAPERS, 1873

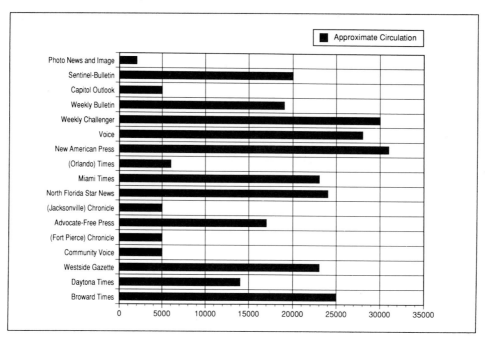

AFRICAN AMERICAN NEWSPAPERS IN FLORIDA

NEWSPAPERS have played an important role in giving readers news, entertainment, and culture. Immigrants from other countries like Germany, Greece, France, and Italy have often had newspapers in this country in their own language, for example, German, Greek, French, and Italian. African Americans also wanted their own newspapers in order to find out the news that was of more interest to them than to white readers.

The **editors** of Florida newspapers after the Civil War had a problem that other southern editors had: reporting all the important news in a community that had many different types of people without driving away those white readers who did not want to know about the nonwhite members of the community. Many white editors chose to ignore the African American community. Others put African American news in separate sections such as "News of the Colored Community" or used headlines indicating in some way that the news was of African Americans, for example "Bicycle Race (Colored)."

To get around this problem, African American leaders dreamed of publishing their own newspapers with news that their readers wanted to hear. This country's first

DISCUSSION TOPICS: As you read this chapter, think about the answers to these questions: 1. What are the advantages of having foreign-language newspapers in the United States for speakers of those languages? 2. What are the advantages and disadvantages of a newspaper compared to television or the radio? 3. Discuss the graph concerning "African American Newspapers in Florida" in terms of which newspapers have the largest circulation, which have the smallest, and which ones serve the same cities.

50

M. M. Lewey
Florida State Archives

African American newspaper, *Freedom's Journal*, which appeared in New York City in 1827, announced an objective that is still important for such newspapers today: "We wish to **plead** our cause. Too long have others spoken for us." The newspaper was the first to use such phrases as "people of color." The first African American newspaper in the South was *L'union*, which began in New Orleans, Louisiana, in 1862.

Until the end of the Civil War in 1865 most African American newspapers were published in the North. There African Americans had more freedom to publish newspapers and were better educated than in the South, where slave owners did not want their slaves to be able to read and write. After the Civil War, many African American newspapers were begun in the South, including Florida. These newspapers encouraged African Americans to vote, to become better educated, and to succeed in business.

Florida produced one of the most famous African-American newspapermen of the 19th century, T. Thomas Fortune, but he published his newspaper in New York City. The first Florida newspaper owned by an African American was Gainesville's *New Era*, which Josiah Walls bought in 1873; Walls was Florida's only Congressman in the U.S. House of Representatives in 1870 (see p. 43).

Walls later joined **Matthew M. Lewey** to publish another newspaper, the *Farmers' Journal*. Lewey established one of the state's more famous African American newspapers, the *Sentinel*, in Gainesville in 1887 and published it for the next 40 years, although he moved it to three different cities; today it is the Tampa *Sentinel-Bulletin*. James Weldon Johnson established a daily African American newspaper in Jacksonville, the *Daily American*.

Today's African Americans in Florida also want to have their own newspapers.

Front page of *The Florida Sentinel*
Florida State Archives

They have established the following newspapers in Florida: *Broward Times* in Coconut Creek, *Daytona Times* in Daytona Beach, *Westside Gazette* in Fort Lauderdale, *Community Voice* in Fort Myers, *Chronicle* in Fort Pierce, (1) *Advocate-Free Press* and (2) *Chronicle* and (3) *North Florida Star News* in Jacksonville, *Miami Times* in Miami, *Times* in Orlando, (1) *New American Press* and (2) *Voice* in Pensacola, *Weekly Challenger* in St.

Petersburg, *Weekly Bulletin* in Sarasota, *Capitol Outlook* in Tallahassee, *Sentinel-Bulletin* in Tampa, and *Photo News and Image* in West Palm Beach.

Further reading:

"Matthew M. Lewey: Florida's First Black Newspaper Editor," in *Twelve Black Floridians* by Leedell W. Neyland (Tallahassee, FL: Florida Agricultural and Mechanical Foundation, 1970), pp. 7-14; Jerrell H. Shofner, "Florida," in *The Black Press in the South, 1865-1979*, edited by Henry Lewis Suggs (Westport, CT: Greenwood Press, 1983), pp. 91-118.

20.
TURPENTINE CAMPS, 1877

Working in the Florida Panhandle
Florida State Archives

MANY AFRICAN AMERICANS WORKED at a very hard job called turpentining. Workers in turpentine camps would cut pine trees, collect the **sap** that came from them, and make it into **turpentine**. The men who worked in such camps were like slaves.

One way that southern states like Florida could raise money was to allow private companies to hire prisoners to work in turpentine camps. This was called the **convict-lease system**. It began in Florida in 1877 and allowed whites to force African Americans back into a kind of slavery. Under

this system, laws were passed which made it easy for the police to arrest poor people, especially African Americans, and send them to work in the terrible conditions of the turpentine camps.

In those camps the workers had to work as quickly as possible from morning to night. Armed guards chained the workers to their beds at night to prevent them from escaping. If the prisoners became sick or injured on the job, they suffered and sometimes died because no doctors were there to help them. If the guards thought prisoners deserved punishment, they would **flog** them

DISCUSSION TOPICS: As you read this chapter, think about the answers to these questions: 1. Do you know of any movies that show what prison life is like? 2. What are the arguments for and against the death penalty? 3. What are some ways that people try to prevent drunk driving?

or put them in a **sweatbox**, a small box that had no light and no air going through it. Guards also hung prisoners up off the ground by their thumbs, a painful **torture** that caused permanent damage to the thumbs of the prisoners. Prisoners sometimes tried to escape from such terrible camps, but they were usually not strong enough or healthy enough to outrun the dogs used by the guards to track down escaped prisoners.

Desperate prisoners tried to cut them-selves or even kill themselves, but, if they lived, doctors would patch them up and send them back to the camps. Henry Flagler, the man who built a railroad along the east coast of Florida down to Key West, used **convicts** in the 1890s to help build the railroad. The railroad that the men built was so good that it lasted for many years. The legislature finally ended the convict-lease system in 1923 after many citizens demanded that the system end.

Working on turpentine
Courtesy, Tampa-Hillsborough County Public Library System

Further reading:
John C. Powell, *The American Siberia or Fourteen Years Experience in a Southern Convict Camp* (Gainesville: University of Florida Press, 1976).

21.
FLORIDA AGRICULTURAL & MECHANICAL UNIVERSITY (FAMU), 1887

Thomas Tucker, first president of Florida State Normal and Industrial School.
Florida State Archives

ON OCTOBER 3, 1887, the Florida State Legislature established in Tallahassee the State Normal College for Colored Students. The purpose of the school was to train African American teachers for schools throughout Florida. The school began with 15 students in 1887, but slowly got bigger and bigger until now it has over 9,000 students.

The first president of the school was Thomas DeSaille Tucker, a man from Sierra Leone in Africa. He served as president for 13 years, during which time the school grew from one building to eight and from 15 students to 159. The next president, who began serving in 1901, was Nathan B. Young.

In 1909, the school became a four-year college and was called Florida Agricultural and Mechanical College. In 1953, it was renamed Florida A & M University and became part of the Florida state university system, a system that now includes ten public universities. While many students at FAMU come from other states, approximately 68%

DISCUSSION TOPICS: As you read this chapter, think about the answers to these questions: 1. What strengths does a school like FAMU offer African American students? 2. If you were going to establish a Black Archives Research Center and Museum, what would you include in the collection? 3. Look at the graph about the four African American schools in Florida; if the total number of students who attend all four schools is 50,000, how many attend each school?

> ## VOCABULARY
> Sierra Leone, Frederick S. Humphries, Black Archives Research Center and Museum

55

Florida State Normal Class of 1904
Florida State Archives

of its students are from Florida.

Frederick S. Humphries, president of FAMU since 1985 and the winner of many honors, won the 1990 Thurgood Marshall Educational Achievement Award for his many contributions to education. He helped FAMU

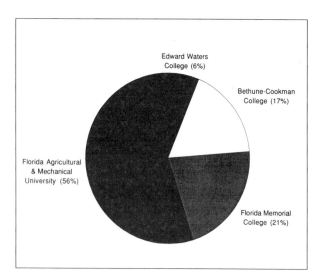

The 1989 Enrollment in African American Colleges and Universities in Florida

become one of the most successful universities in the nation in attracting National Achievement Scholars, African American high school students who score highest on the Scholastic Assessment Test. In fact, in 1992, more of the country's best African American high school seniors chose FAMU than any other university.

Among the buildings on campus, and one that is on the Florida Black Heritage Trail, is the **Black Archives Research Center and Museum** in the Carnegie Library Building. Over 100,000 people a year visit this building, the oldest on the campus, to see the collection of material about African Americans in Florida. We will discuss the university in more detail in Chapters 33, 38, and 39.

Further reading:
Leedell W. Neyland & John W. Riley, *The History of Florida Agricultural and Mechanical University* (Gainesville: University of Florida Press, 1963).

22.
SPORTS IN FLORIDA, 1890

SPORTS HAVE ALWAYS BEEN an important part of life in America. Many young men and women have used their athletic ability to help their schools, make their families proud, and earn good salaries as professional athletes. In the late 1800s, people would often go out to the local ballpark and watch their friends and neighbors play other teams in football, baseball, and basketball.

Football teams like the team from the Dunbar High School in Quincy, Florida, pictured on page 58 played against other teams. Baseball was a particular favorite in the summer, although the heat and humidity

Two Palm Beach baseball teams: the Royal Poinciana Hotel Team, 1915-16 (top) and the Breakers Hotel Team, 1914 (bottom)
National Baseball Library, Cooperstown, NY

DISCUSSION TOPICS: As you read this chapter, think about the answers to these questions: 1. Why do you think Florida has produced so many good African American athletes? 2. What part have sports played in the history of Florida? 3. Many athletes become sports announcers when they have finished playing their sport professionally. What are the advantages of such people becoming announcers?

VOCABULARY
major league teams,
Negro Leagues, segregation,
Florida Sports Hall of Fame

A football team at Quincy's Dunbar School
Florida State Archives

of the South kept many teams away, especially the **major league teams**. What the South did produce, however, was a number of great African American baseball stars who became famous, if not rich, by playing in the **Negro Leagues**.

Confederate veterans and ex-slaves who had learned how to play baseball from Union soldiers during the Civil War brought baseball to many communities in the South. When baseball became popular in America in the 1800s, African Americans began playing the sport, but they had to have their own teams because they were not allowed to play on white teams. The practice of **segregation** kept the races apart.

Among the Florida cities which had good African American baseball teams in the 1890s were Jacksonville and Miami. Jacksonville had African American teams like the Roman Cities and the Red Caps. In 1897, 10 of the 40 baseball teams in Jacksonville were African American. Some Florida hotels had African American teams, like the teams pictured on page 57.

Many towns in Southern states, including Florida, had African American baseball teams that competed against other such teams. Going out to the ballpark to see the local team play a team from another town was fun and allowed the whole family to take part as spectators. In the days before radio, television, and air conditioning, watching a baseball game on a summer evening was a popular entertainment. A winning team gave the town pride in its players.

Life was not easy for the players on those African American baseball teams, especially when they had to travel to other towns to play ball. Players spent much of their time traveling from town to town in order to play the games. Their pay was small. Sometimes they had to play three or four games in a single day in order to earn enough money to make it worthwhile.

Sometimes the African American teams

John Henry "Pop" Lloyd
National Baseball Library, Cooperstown, NY

from the South would play the white teams from the major leagues; if the African American team won, as it sometimes did, that thrilled their hometown fans.

One of the best players in the Negro Leagues, John Henry Lloyd, was born in Palatka, Florida, on April 25, 1884. Some newspaper reporters and fans compared Lloyd, who is pictured here, to the great Honus Wagner, one of the greatest shortstops in the history of white baseball. When Lloyd played baseball in Cuba, the Cubans called him "Cuchara" or "shovel" because his big hands were able to scoop up any ball hit near him. Lloyd was voted into the Baseball Hall of Fame in 1977.

After the great Jackie Robinson became the first African American to play in the major leagues in 1947, many skilled players from the Negro Leagues joined white teams. Among the professional baseball players from Florida who are in the **Florida Sports Hall of Fame** in Lake City are Andre Dawson, Hal McRae, and Tim Raines.

Further Reading:

John B. Holway, *Blackball Stars: Negro League Pioneers* (Westport, CT: Meckler, 1988). *Black Diamonds: Life in the Negro Leagues from the Men Who Lived It* (Westport, CT: Meckler, 1989). Robert Peterson, *Only the Ball Was White: A History of Legendary Black Players and All-black Professional Teams* (New York: McGraw-Hill, 1984).

Honus Wagner (1874-1955), one of the greatest shortstops in the history of white baseball, once commented about Lloyd: "They called John Henry Lloyd 'The Black Wagner,' and I was anxious to see him play. Well, one day I had an opportunity to go see him play, and after I saw him I felt honored that they would name such a great player after me."

23.

MARY MCLEOD BETHUNE, 1875-1955

Mary McLeod Bethune
Florida State Archives

HOLDING THE BOOK UPSIDE DOWN, the young Mary Jane pretended to read it. She wanted to go to school to learn how to read more than anything in the world. But Mary Jane's family was poor, and none of her older brothers and sisters attended school. She begged and begged until finally her mother agreed to let her go to the mission school in Sumter County, South Carolina. This was the beginning of a life devoted to learning and to teaching others.

DISCUSSION TOPICS: As you read this chapter, think about the answers to these questions: 1. Do you think that schools should give scholarships to students who are poor or just to smart students, regardless of how much money they have? 2. If you were the mayor of a large city, how would you try to get rid of the slums in the city? 3. Look at the photograph on page 62 entitled "Gathering Watermelons." Discuss it in terms of the time of year, who does what kind of work, and methods of carrying the watermelons.

Mary Jane McLeod Bethune, Florida's most famous African American, was born on July 10, 1875, in Mayesville, South Carolina. When she was very young, she and her 16 brothers and sisters helped their parents, who had been slaves, farm their five acres of land. Mary Jane was a hard worker. Instead of playing games and having fun all day, she worked long hours picking cotton and harvesting vegetables on the family farm. After working in the fields all day, Mary Jane did her household chores.

When Mary Jane was seven years old, she attended a mission school taught by Miss Emma Wilson. Mary Jane's dream of learning

---

VOCABULARY
scholarship, slums, homeless, educator, racism, discrimination

---

60

to read was about to come true. Because there was no school bus for her to ride to school, she walked five miles to school and another five miles home each day. She was such a good student that, after graduating from the mission school, she won a **scholarship** in 1887 to attend Scotia Seminary in North Carolina.

Leaving all of her family and friends behind, Mary Jane must have been scared. She was only 12 years old when she took a train to her new school in North Carolina. She did not know then that it would be five years before she saw her family again. At her new school Mary Jane, who worked to pay for her room and food, did chores that were very similar to her household chores. She enjoyed school, especially English and music. At one point she decided that she wanted to become a teacher and a missionary to Africa.

Mary Jane graduated from Scotia Seminary in 1894 and won another scholarship to the Moody Bible Institute in Chicago, Illinois, a school that would train her to become a missionary. She was the only African American at Moody, but she learned there that the color of a person's skin was not important. She spent much of her time trying to help others. She visited prisoners and read the Bible and sang songs to them and also worked in **slums** and with the **homeless**. After all of her hard work and preparation to serve as a missionary in Africa, she was very disappointed when she learned that there was no missionary position for her.

Even though she was disappointed, she knew that millions of people in the United States needed help also, especially African Americans. She therefore returned to her hometown and taught school there for a year before taking a job at Haines Institute in Augusta, Georgia, in 1896. Mary Jane spent a year at Haines Institute, teaching African American boys and girls in the eighth grade. She then went to Kindell Institute near her family home in Mayesville, South Carolina, where she was able to share her salary with her family, who were still very poor. She helped to send her two younger sisters to school and helped her parents pay their bills.

Mary McLeod Bethune at Bethune-Cookman College in Daytona Beach, 1943
Florida State Archives

61

Mary Jane, it seems, always put others first.

In May 1898, she married another teacher, Albertus Bethune, and a year later their only child, Albertus, Jr., was born. Six months after the birth of her son, Ms. Bethune was offered a teaching job in Palatka, Florida. She accepted the position, moved to Palatka, and began doing missionary work among the poor and those in jail. She also had a part-time job selling insurance policies for the Afro-American Life Insurance Company.

Ms. Bethune began to dream about opening her own school. She had heard about hundreds of African Americans who were building the Florida East Coast Railroad and knew that their living conditions were not good. She believed that she could help them by opening a school for their children. So, in 1904, Ms. Bethune took her son, Albertus, and moved to Daytona Beach, where she found the conditions there to be worse than she had imagined.

With less than two dollars, Ms. Bethune rented a cottage to be used as her school building and opened Daytona Normal and Industrial Institute for Negro Girls. The five students who attended paid 50 cents a week. Before long more students enrolled. Ms. Bethune did not have a lot of money and asked for help from the African American community, many of whom donated food and money. Several rich white people also helped Ms. Bethune; for example, Mr. James Gamble contributed thousands of dollars to help make Ms. Bethune's dream come true.

Through hard work and determination Ms. Bethune's school grew. She also continued her missionary activities in the African American community. Because it was difficult and sometimes impossible for African Americans to get medical treatment, in 1911 she opened a hospital for them on her campus. This hospital had only two beds at first, but it grew into a 26-bed hospital headed by an African American doctor.

In 1923, Ms. Bethune joined her school with Cookman Institute, a school for boys in Jacksonville, Florida. The new combined school, located in Daytona Beach, became known as Bethune-Cookman Institute. Ms.

Gathering watermelons
Florida State Archives

Bethune's dream had come true. Her one-room school had become a beautiful campus with eight buildings, a large staff, and over 300 students.

Mary McLeod Bethune was well known as an **educator**, but she made a name for herself in other areas also. She was a member of the National Association of Colored Women (NACW), an organization that tried to improve conditions for African Americans in the United States, and in 1924 she was elected president of the NACW. She was also the founder of the National Council of Negro Women and a member and officer of numerous other African American women's clubs.

She spent a lifetime fighting against **racism** and **discrimination** against people of color in this country. She favored prison reform as well as anti-lynching laws and gave speeches all across the country on such issues. Ms. Bethune worked very hard to change the negative image of African Americans held by so many whites to a positive one; her membership in the Commission on Interracial Cooperation went a long way toward improving race relations. In 1935, she received two very special honors: she was named one of the 50 most influential women in the United States, and she received the Spingarn Award from the National Association for the Advancement of Colored People (NAACP), which was given to the African American "who shall have reached the highest achievement in his field of activity."

Ms. Bethune's reputation and influence continued to grow. Presidents Calvin Coolidge and Herbert Hoover appointed her to several important positions. In 1935, she became a member of President Franklin D. Roosevelt's African American "brain trust." The following year Roosevelt appointed Ms. Bethune director of the National Youth Administration's Division of Negro Affairs, and she became the first African American woman to head a federal agency.

Ms. Bethune's relationship with the president's wife, Eleanor, and her membership in the Black Cabinet placed her in a position to inform the president and others about the conditions of African Americans in the United States and the racism that they had to deal with on a daily basis. She worked hard to have Congress provide money to improve housing and education for African Americans and even led demonstrations against businesses that discriminated against those with darker skin.

Mary McLeod Bethune died in May 1955 at the age of 79 after a lifetime of helping others. With her strong determination and faith she had improved the lives of many men and women. She was a woman who never gave up, who was not afraid to dream and to make her dreams come true, who believed that everything was possible with faith. Starting with less than two dollars she began a college in Daytona Beach and improved conditions for African Americans. In her drive to improve race relations in this country, she was not afraid to speak out against injustices, and she convinced many whites to change their views about African Americans. In 1985, the United States government recognized the contributions of Ms. Bethune, an African American woman of courage and conviction, when it issued a postage stamp in her honor.

Further reading:
Malu Halasa, *Mary McLeod Bethune: Educator* (New York: Chelsea House Publishers, 1989).

24.

ABRAMS L. LEWIS AND THE AFRO-AMERICAN LIFE INSURANCE COMPANY

ABRAMS LINCOLN LEWIS, one of the founders of the Afro-American Life Insurance Company, was born to poor parents in Madison, Florida, in 1865, the year the Civil War ended. His family moved to Jacksonville when he was a young boy, but they were too poor to send him to school. Even though he was disappointed that he could not go to school, he did not feel sorry for himself. Instead, he found a job as a water boy in a Jacksonville lumber mill and began to save his money.

For over 20 years, Abrams worked at the lumber mill, where he was regarded as a "trusted and highly respected employee." Even though he started out as a water boy, he advanced to the position of **foreman** and received the highest salary paid to any African American working at the mill. He continued to save his money and, at age 23, made

a wise investment when he bought part of the first shoe store owned and operated by African Americans in Jacksonville.

Mr. Lewis was involved in many social and **humanitarian** activities in Jacksonville. In fact, it was through fraternal organizations such as the Sons and Daughters of Jacob and the Masonic Lodge that he sharpened his business skills. For example, serving as the treasurer of the insurance department of the Masonic Order taught him a lot about the insurance business. In January 1901, Mr. Lewis and six other African Americans contributed $100 each and formed an insurance company, the Afro-American Industrial and Benefit Association. This was an important undertaking, because it was very difficult for African Americans to buy insurance at that time from white companies.

Mr. Lewis was the first treasurer of this new business. The seven founders were able to provide low-cost health and burial **insurance** to poor African Americans and make a profit at the same time. Eighteen years later, Mr. Lewis was named president of the company, which had changed its name to the Afro-American Insurance Company; under his leadership the company continued to

---

DISCUSSION TOPICS: As you read this chapter, think about the answers to these questions: 1. If you were going to own a store, what kind of store would it be and why? 2. Even if life insurance and car insurance do not play a major part in your life, you protect yourself from harm in other ways. For example, when playing sports, what do you do to make sure you do not receive a serious injury? 3. Do you think that anyone who wants to go to college should be given the money to do so? If they cannot repay the money, what kind of work should they be required to do to pay back the school or government that gave them the money?

VOCABULARY
foreman, humanitarian, insurance, poverty

Men operating machinery in a mill
Courtesy, Tampa-Hillsborough County Public Library System

expand and grow. By 1947 the Afro-American Insurance Company was worth approximately $1,500,000. In addition to being an owner of the Afro-American Insurance Company, he was also a founding member of both the Negro Business League and the Negro Insurance Association.

Through hard work and determination, Mr. Lewis became one of the richest African Americans in the South. He shared his good fortunes with others and attempted to improve conditions for African Americans in Jacksonville. One way he did this was by helping to establish the Lincoln Golf and Country Club for African Americans. Since he had been unable to attend school, Mr. Lewis made contributions to African American colleges in Florida and provided scholarships to many students. He was very proud when Wilberforce University in Ohio awarded him an honorary degree in 1936.

Mr. Lewis never gave up and did not allow **poverty** or racism to keep him from improving himself. He had faith, worked hard, and did very well in the business world. When he died in 1947, he left a wonderful example for others to follow and a strong insurance company that provided a service to thousands of people.

Further reading:

Leedell W. Neyland, *Twelve Black Floridians* (Tallahassee: Florida Agricultural and Mechanical University Foundation, 1970).

25.
AUGUSTA SAVAGE, SCULPTOR
1900-1962

Girls posed in Gainesville with their toys
Florida State Archives

AUGUSTA SAVAGE EARNED an outstanding reputation as a **sculptor**. Born in Green Cove Springs, Florida, on February 29, 1900, Augusta was the seventh of 14 children.

DISCUSSION TOPICS: As you read this chapter, think about the answers to these questions: 1. If you were going to have busts of famous people in your home, which people would you choose? 2. Do you think a sculptor should produce a bust that looks exactly like the person, or should the sculptor put in only the person's good features? 3. Augusta Savage's father would have preferred that Augusta play with dolls, as the girls in the photograph above are doing, rather than make models from clay. What can children learn from playing with dolls? Also look at the photograph on page 67 of the two women working a garden patch. How do you think the soil in such a garden patch differs from the soil that Augusta used to make models?

When she was a young girl, she played outdoors and made ducks and other animal shapes from the red clay found outside her house. Her father, a minister, disapproved of this and considered it "foolishness." Making "graven images," as he called them, was against his religious principles and so he punished her for making models from the red clay. She did not want to disobey him, but she enjoyed her art work so much that it was difficult for her to stop. She even played hookey from school to practice her art and soon learned to hide her art work from her father.

VOCABULARY
sculptor, pottery, potter, bust,
sculptures, finances

Women tilling the soil in front of poor shacks.
P.K. Yonge Library of Florida History, University of Florida

In 1915, Augusta moved with her parents to West Palm Beach, Florida. There was no red clay there, but she found a **pottery** store and begged the **potter** for clay. Augusta continued to shape models of animals and people from clay and sold pieces of her art work to people who passed by, while other children sold lemonade from roadside stands. One man liked her work so much that he convinced her to display it at the county fair. She did so and won a prize for best exhibit, selling a few pieces of art as well. One of her pieces on display was a **bust** of Henry M. Flagler, the man who helped build the railroad along the east coast of Florida down to Key West.

Friends encouraged her to go north, but Augusta went first to Jacksonville, where she hoped to earn a living by making **sculptures** of successful African Americans. This, however, did not work out, and at age 21 she arrived in New York City with only $4.60 in her pocket. Augusta was so determined to become a sculptor that she worked as a maid by day and attended art classes at night. Her hard work finally began to pay off.

She won a scholarship to the Cooper's Union Woman's Art School and began her first formal training in sculpture. She was very happy in 1923 when she learned that she had won a competition over many white students and was awarded a scholarship to study in

France. Her happiness soon turned to tears when the scholarship was taken away because she was an African American. It was common during that time to judge African Americans by their skin color and not their talents.

But Augusta won another competition in 1925. That time, although the color of her skin did not keep her from accepting a scholarship to study at the Royal Academy of Fine Arts in Rome, Italy, her **finances** did. She was supposed to pay her own transportation to Italy, but she had no money.

In 1929, Augusta received a $1500 Julius Rosenwald Fellowship to study in Paris for two years. The National Urban League of New York bought clothes for her. Augusta won many awards for her work in Paris.

After returning to the United States, she received praise for many of her sculptures, which included *The Head of Dr. Du Bois, Lift Every Voice and Sing,* and *Gamin.* Ms. Savage later opened an art school to train others in sculpturing, helped organize the Harlem Artist Guild, and directed the Harlem Community Art Center. She died in 1962 after a distinguished career as a sculptor.

Further reading:
Lottie Montgomery Clark, "Negro Women Leaders of Florida," M.A. Thesis, The Florida State University, 1947; Augusta Savage, "An Autobiography" *Crisis* 36 (August 1929), p. 269.

26.

THE
CENTRAL LIFE INSURANCE COMPANY

Portrait of African American bricklayers
Florida State Archives

THE CENTRAL LIFE INSURANCE COMPANY was founded in Tampa, Florida, in 1922, when African American business and professional men and women began to meet the needs of African Americans in south Florida. With $10,000, such people as W.D. Potter (the editor and owner of the *Tampa Bulletin*), George S. Middleton (Tampa's only African American postal clerk), **physicians** L. A. Howell, T. L. Lowrie, and S.J. Johnson, dentist C. H. Norton, educator Mary McLeod Bethune, and others organized the company. It was able to expand quickly and by 1935 was conducting business in almost every Florida city. It also provided **employment** for over 300 men and women. By 1935 more than one million dollars had been paid in **claims.**

DISCUSSION TOPICS: As you read this chapter, think about the answers to these questions: 1. Why is it often better for ten persons to raise money for a project than just one? 2. Why is it sometimes not better? 3. How do the different occupations pictured in the photographs in this chapter (bricklayers, road workers, mail carrier) differ in terms of work hours, salary, and safety?

VOCABULARY
physicians, employment, claims

68

Building a road in Tampa
Courtesy, Tampa-Hillsborough County Public Library System

A Jacksonville mail carrier in 1887
Florida State Archives

27.
CLARA FRYE, NURSE, 1872-1937

Clara Frye
The Tampa Tribune

CLARA FRYE WAS FLORIDA'S most famous African American nurse. Born in New York in 1872, Clara was the daughter of a southern African American man and a white woman from England. When Clara was ten years old, her family moved to Montgomery, Alabama. She dreamed of becoming a nurse and, when she was old enough, she went to Chicago to attend nursing school. After finishing nursing school, she moved back to Montgomery,

where she practiced nursing for 16 years.

In 1908, Ms. Frye moved to Tampa, Florida, and very soon became known as "the best **fever** nurse" in the city. Ms. Frye was so upset because there was no hospital for doctors to treat the sick that she rented a building on Lamar Avenue and opened a hospital. Both African Americans and whites helped her buy the property. A few years later, the hospital burned down, but Ms. Frye used the insurance money to rebuild it.

Both African American and white patients were admitted to the hospital where they were treated by both African American and white doctors. Ms. Frye made very little

---

DISCUSSION TOPICS: As you read this chapter, think about the answers to these questions: 1. How do you think hospitals should protect their nurses and doctors from a disease like AIDS? 2. If you were dying from an incurable disease, where would you like to die? 3. What dangers could the women in the photographs here (the shrimp factory and the flower field) suffer in their workplace?

VOCABULARY
fever, wing, pavilion

Women in the shrimp industry in Apalachicola
Courtesy, Tampa-Hillsborough County Public Library System

money from her hospital and sometimes could not pay her own bills, but she never turned anyone away, even those who could not afford to pay. In 1930-31, the city of Tampa took over Ms. Frye's hospital and changed the name to Municipal Hospital for Negroes.

Clara Frye died in poverty in 1937, but her contribution to the city did not go unnoticed. The mayor of Tampa called Ms. Frye one of Tampa's outstanding citizens, and when a new medical building for African Americans was built in 1938, it was named the Clara Frye Municipal Negro Hospital. In 1991, Tampa General Hospital renamed a nine-floor patient-care **wing** the Clara Frye **Pavilion** in honor of this unselfish, caring woman.

Workers in a gladiola field
Courtesy, Tampa-Hilsborough County Public Library System

Further reading:
Lottie Montgomery Clark, "Negro Women Leaders of Florida," M.A. Thesis, The Florida State University, 1947; *The Tampa Tribune*, February 24, 1991.

28.

EARTHA MARY MAGDALENE WHITE, "ANGEL OF MERCY," 1876-1974

EARTHA MARY MAGDALENE WHITE has been called an "angel of mercy" because of her unselfish efforts to make life better for African Americans in Jacksonville. Born in Jacksonville in 1876, Eartha attended the Florida Baptist Academy and spent most of her summers in New York with her mother, who worked aboard a cruise ship; Eartha took beauty culture classes while her mother worked.

One day a white woman whose hair Eartha was working on heard her singing and remarked that she had a beautiful voice. It may have been that compliment that convinced Eartha to enroll at the National Conservatory of Music in New York, where she studied under the famous Harry T. Burleigh. While studying there, she also sang with the Oriental-American Opera Company.

When Eartha became engaged to be married, she thought her life would become even more complete, but, only one month before her wedding, her **fiancé** died. At that point she decided that she would never marry, but would devote her life to working for God.

Eartha returned to Jacksonville in 1896. During the Spanish-American War between

Eartha M. M. White
Eartha M. M. White Collection, Thomas G. Carpenter Library, University of North Florida

Spain and the United States (1898) she helped to nurse sick soldiers. After the war, while teaching in a poor country school in Duval County, she managed to improve conditions in the school and convinced the county to

DISCUSSION TOPICS: As you read this chapter, think about the answers to these questions: 1. If a fire were destroying your home and you had only ten minutes to save objects (all the people are safe), what would you save? Why? 2. What are some ways you can think of to encourage people to register to vote and then to vote? 3. The family pictured in the sketch on page 73 may not be able to afford good health care. What might a visiting health-care worker suggest to such a family to make the home safer?

> *VOCABULARY*
> fiancé, social worker, Depression, orphanage, tuberculosis, correctional institution

A simple meal in 1885
Florida State Archives

build a new two-room building; she later transferred to Stanton School in 1901. In addition to teaching, Ms. White worked part-time for the Afro-American Life Insurance Company. She was the first woman to work for that company and the one who saved the company's records during the terrible 1901 Jacksonville fire.

That fire, which destroyed much of Jacksonville, had a major effect on the city's African American community. Many African Americans lost their homes, as well as their food, clothing, and shelter. The Jacksonville fire began Ms. White's career as a **social worker** in the African American community. She became involved in the relief efforts and helped to start the Union Benevolent Association, a charitable organization that soon made her its president. Along with her mother, Clara White, she collected money to build a home for the elderly, which she opened in 1902. Ms.

White played a major role in organizing the City Federation of Women's Clubs, an organization that performed many charitable activities in the African American community.

With very little money, Ms. White in 1922 opened the Clara White Mission and tried to meet most of the needs of poor African Americans, especially during the great **Depression**, a time when many people lost their jobs and homes. Thousands of African Americans found food, clothing, and shelter at the Clara White Mission. The mission also operated an **orphanage**, as well as a day nursery to care for the children of working mothers. Ms. White was also responsible for getting the first playground built in the African American community. The mission became a community center where many cultural events were held. Every Christmas Ms. White provided a decorated tree and gifts for the poor.

Ms. White spent many hours working in the African American neighborhoods. She helped secure a **tuberculosis** rest home for African Americans in 1936 and helped in prison reform. She visited prisoners in jail and tried to help them turn their lives around. She was responsible for getting officials to improve facilities in the African American section of the Duval County Prison and in 1942 convinced the Florida Legislature to build a **correctional institution** for young girls, who had often been jailed with adult women.

Her leadership ability and influence among both African Americans and whites were recognized by many, and she was appointed to several important committees. For example, the governor of Florida named her to the War Camp Community Service Committee and to the Farm and Food Conservation Committee. She served on Florida's National Defense Council for Negroes and ran the largest Red Cross Unit in Jacksonville.

Ms. White joined Mary McLeod Bethune and Blanche Armwood in fighting racism and discrimination. She encouraged African Ameri-cans to register to vote; in 1920 she served cold lemonade to African American women who were standing in long lines to register to vote in the hot Florida sun. Ms. White also denounced lynching and was a founding member and director of the Florida Anti-Lynching Crusaders Committee. She was also a member of the National Association of Colored Women as well as the National Association for the Advancement of Colored People (NAACP). It was a proud moment for her when she attended the civil rights march on Washington in 1963, a march that another Floridian, A. Philip Randolph, helped organize. Ms. White spent much of her life serving as a bridge between Jacksonville's African Americans and whites.

By the time of her death in 1974, Ms. White had received numerous awards for her efforts. She was an honored guest at the White House twice. In 1986, 12 years after her death, Florida officials made Eartha Mary Magdalene White a member of the Florida Women's Hall of Fame, a fitting memorial for a woman who had done so much for the state's African Americans.

Further reading:

Charles E. Bennett, *Twelve on the River St. Johns* (Jacksonville: University of North Florida Press, 1989), pp. 137-148; Leedell W. Neyland, *Twelve Black Floridians* (Tallahassee: Florida Agricultural and Mechanical University Foundation, 1970); Lottie Montgomery Clark, "Negro Women Leaders of Florida," M.A. Thesis, The Florida State University, 1947; James B. Crooks, *Jacksonville After the Fire, 1901-1919: A New South City* (Jacksonville: University of North Florida Press, 1991).

29.

JAMES WELDON JOHNSON, AUTHOR, COMPOSER, DIPLOMAT, CIVIL RIGHTS LEADER, 1871-1938

JAMES WELDON JOHNSON is one of Florida's most famous African Americans. He was a well-rounded man and did well as an administrator, author, **composer**, poet, **diplomat**, **attorney**, scholar, and civil rights leader.

James Weldon was born in Jacksonville, Florida, June 17, 1871. His parents worked hard to provide a decent life for James and his brother, J. Rosamond Johnson; their father worked as head waiter at the St. James Hotel, and their mother taught school. The parents made sure there were books and music in their home, and their mother taught her sons how to play the piano. She also read to them before bedtime, choosing such books as *David Copperfield* and *Tales of a Grandfather*. When James Weldon learned how to read, his father gave him a seven-volume set of books which included *Peter and his Pony* and *Willie Wilson the Newsboy*. He treasured them all.

James Weldon enjoyed playing tops and marbles, but baseball was his favorite game. He played pitcher for a team called the Domestics and developed a very good curve ball. Not only was James Weldon a good player, but he also became an expert about professional baseball teams and players. His favorite team was the Detroits.

After graduating from Stanton Grade School, James Weldon attended Atlanta University in Georgia and graduated with honors in 1894. He returned to Jacksonville and became an administrator. He became principal of Stanton, his old school, and turned it into an outstanding institution when he

James Weldon Johnson
Florida State Archives

DISCUSSION TOPICS: This chapter presents one of Florida's most distinguished African Americans, James Weldon Johnson, and discusses various jobs that he held, for example principal of a school, composer, attorney, consul, and diplomat. As you read this chapter, think about the answers to these questions: 1. What makes a good principal of a school? 2. If you were composing a song about African Americans, what would you include? 3. Discuss the different musical instruments in the photograph on page 76 in terms of difficulty of playing, ease of carrying, etc.

A Tampa band
Florida State Archives

helped it become a high school.

He also began to prepare for a career in law. In those days a person could read or study law with an attorney instead of attending law school. Mr. Thomas Ledwith of Jacksonville agreed to let James Weldon read and prepare for the law with him. James Weldon studied so hard that he became the first African American in Florida to qualify for the **bar** through an open examination in a state court.

In a crowded courtroom, James Weldon Johnson passed a difficult oral exam given by prominent Jacksonville attorneys E. J. L'Engle, Major W. B. Young, and Duncan U. Fletcher. Major Young, however, appeared to be upset that an African American had done so well and angrily walked out of the courtroom. After James Weldon was admitted to the Florida bar, he opened a law office with a friend and practiced law part-time for a few years.

In the meantime, his brother, J. Rosamond, had returned to Jacksonville from New York City, where he had learned about the musical and theatrical world of a big city. He excited James Weldon with his many stories about Broadway, and before long they were writing songs, musicals, and operas and spending their summers in New York.

The brothers wrote a song that many of us are familiar with. In 1900, in honor of Abraham Lincoln's birthday, James Weldon wrote what we now call "Lift Ev'ry Voice and Sing." J. Rosamond set it to music, and 500 African American school children sang it at the Lincoln celebration in Jacksonville. It is now recognized all over the country as the Negro National Anthem.

After an incident where James Weldon was almost lynched for being with an African American woman who looked white, and after a fire that destroyed Stanton High School,

76

the brothers decided to leave Jacksonville for good. They went to New York City and began a successful career composing musicals and operas. In addition to the work he did with his brother, he also wrote novels and poems. James Weldon Johnson became a well-known author. "The Creation" is one of his poems that many students learn in school.

In 1906, President Theodore Roosevelt appointed James Weldon Johnson United States **consul** to Venezuela. He served in this position until 1909, when he was appointed United States consul to Nicaragua. Johnson finally resigned from the State Department in 1912 and returned to writing. But writing occupied only part of his time. He became more and more involved in the cause of African Americans and in 1916 became field secretary for the National Association for the Advancement of Colored People (NAACP).

As field secretary, Johnson began to organize more branches of the NAACP in the South, a part of the country that had only three branches in 1916. In 1917, Johnson visited several Southern cities, including Tampa, Florida, and by 1919 there were more than 130 branches of the NAACP in the South. In 1919-20, Johnson became the first African American to serve as **executive secretary** of the NAACP.

As executive secretary, Johnson wanted to do something about the number of African Americans who were being lynched and killed by whites. After beating, hanging, and cutting up African Americans, these whites were generally not even arrested or punished. Johnson worked hard to secure the passage of a federal anti-lynching bill and persuaded Congressman L. C. Dyer of Missouri to help him.

In 1921, Congressman Dyer introduced the Dyer Anti-Lynching Bill before Congress.

For almost two years, Johnson talked to many congressmen and senators trying to get them to vote for the bill. The bill passed in the House of Representatives, but was defeated in the Senate. Even though the measure did not pass, it brought the horrible crime of lynching to the attention of the American people. Johnson believed that the Dyer Anti-Lynching Bill played a major role in reducing the number of lynchings.

In 1925, the NAACP recognized Johnson's accomplishments as an author, diplomat, and public servant by awarding him the Spingarn Award, its highest honor. The Spingarn Award was given by the NAACP to the African American "who shall have reached the highest achievement in his field of activity." He was also very proud of the Harmon Award, which he received for writing "God's Trombones: Seven Negro Sermons in Verse."

Johnson left the NAACP after 14 years of service to take a teaching position at Fisk University in Nashville, Tennessee, but he did not cut his ties with the NAACP completely; he was elected to its **board of trustees** and made a vice-president. At Fisk, Johnson helped aspiring young African American students to develop their writing skills and prepared them to fight racism.

Johnson represented Florida and African Americans well both nationally and internationally. In the process he was often a victim of prejudice, but he did not let racism and discrimination get the best of him. He fought them head on and tried to encourage others to join the fight. He died in an automobile accident in Maine in 1928 and thus brought to an end a varied and distinguished career.

Further reading:
James Weldon Johnson, *Along This Way: The Autobiography of James Weldon Johnson* (New York: Viking Press, 1968); Ellen Tarry, *Young Jim: The Early Years of James Weldon Johnson* (New York: Dodd, Mead, 1967).

30.
ZORA NEALE HURSTON,
AUTHOR, ANTHROPOLOGIST, FOLKLORIST,
1891-1960

ZORA NEALE HURSTON WAS BORN in the all-African American Community of Eatonville, Florida, not far from Orlando. There is some confusion concerning the year that Zora was born. She claimed that she was born in 1901, but **census** records list her birth year as 1891. Zora grew up in a town that was completely governed by African Americans: the mayor, police chief, and city council were all African American.

Zora loved living in Eatonville. She liked picking oranges, tangerines, and grapefruits from the trees in her yard and swimming in the nearby lake. Sometimes she got into fights with her playmates. Her father thought that Zora was too spirited, but her mother encouraged her to "jump at de sun."

Zora had a vivid imagination. As a young girl she heard many wonderful stories from her friends and relatives. These stories, many of which had been passed from one generation to another, influenced her writings.

Eventually, Zora left her hometown to attend various schools. She graduated from

Zora Neale Hurston
Florida State Archives

DISCUSSION TOPICS: As you read this chapter, think about the answers to these questions: 1. What do you think Zora's mother meant when she told Zora to "jump at de sun"? 2. What parts of your town's history do you think should be in a play or novel some day? 3. What words would you want on your gravestone someday?

VOCABULARY
census, anthropologist, folklore, stroke

The house in St. Augustine where Zora Neale Hurston lived
Kevin M. McCarthy

Barnard College with a degree in the subject of anthropology, which is the study of humanity. Her teacher was Franz Boas, a very famous **anthropologist**. Zora also collected African American **folklore** under Professor Boas' direction.

Zora was a happy person and fun to be around. She loved parties and liked to dance. She loved to wear hats and wore pants at a time when very few women dared. She lived in New York City and was a part of a movement called the Harlem Renaissance. This was a time during the 1920s when many African American authors, playwrights, artists, and poets became famous for their literature. Zora wrote several short stories and plays. In 1925, one of her plays, "Color Struck," won second prize in a competition.

Zora Neale Hurston also wrote some books: *Jonah's Gourd Vine* (1934), *Mules and Men* (1935), *Their Eyes Were Watching God* (1937), *Tell My Horse* (1938), *Moses, Man of the Mountain* (1939), and an autobiography: *Dust Tracks on a Road* (1942). Zora's outgoing personality, the stories that

she had heard as a child, her imagination, and her ability to tell a story all contributed to her literary genius.

Sadly, Zora made very little money from her books. Much of the time she earned just enough to get by. In Florida she lived in St. Augustine while she taught school there. She also worked as a maid, a reporter, and a librarian just to make ends meet. This meant that she could not concentrate on what she really enjoyed: writing. Her health was not good, either. After suffering a **stroke**, Zora unwillingly entered the St. Lucie County welfare home in October 1959. She died three months later.

It is unfortunate that Zora Neale Hurston did not receive much attention for her plays, short stories, and books while she was alive. She was too independent to ask for help from her friends or relatives, and she did not want anyone to feel sorry for her. She enjoyed life to its fullest and made a great contribution to American literature. Zora has recently been rediscovered, and her books are now being widely read.

For more about the town where she was born (Eatonville) and its Zora Neale Hurston Memorial Park, see #33 on the Florida Black Heritage Trail (p. 156). For more about the Fort Pierce house where she lived, see #41 (p. 157). She is buried in a cemetery on 17th Street in Fort Pierce: the Garden of Heavenly Rest. The gravestone, which novelist Alice Walker had put there, reads

Zora Neale Hurston
A Genius of the South
1901 - 1960
Novelist, Folklorist
Anthropologist

Fort Pierce: Gravesite of Zora Neale Hurston
Kevin M. McCarthy

Further reading:

Zora Neale Hurston, *Dust Tracks on a Road* (Chicago: University of Illinois Press, 1984); Robert E. Hemenway, *Zora Neale Hurston: A Literary Biography* (University of Illinois Press, 1980).

31.
THE OCOEE RIOT, 1920

Christina, Florida
Courtesy, Tampa-Hillsborough County Public Library System

AFRICAN AMERICANS WERE OFTEN not allowed to vote in many areas in the South. Sometimes whites would use violence against them if they tried to vote. On November 2, 1920, in Ocoee, Florida, a small town near Orlando, African Americans went to the **polls** to vote. Even though they were only exercising their **constitutional rights**, whites were upset and attacked them.

The section of town that African Americans lived in was destroyed. Houses and churches were burned. An NAACP investigator reported that two African American churches and 25 homes were set on fire and destroyed. In addition, many African Americans were killed. The investigator estimated that 30 people died. One African American who fought to defend his family and property was July Perry, who ended up killing two white men who were trying to harm him;

DISCUSSION TOPICS: As you read this chapter, think about the answers to these questions and points: 1. Many African Americans wanted to live in a town like Eatonville, where everyone was African American. Another such planned town near Lakeland was Christina, Florida, pictured here. What are the advantages and disadvantages of living in a town that is all of one race? 2. If African Americans were not killed by gangs, they were sometimes put in prison for minor crimes. Some of those prisoners found themselves on chain gangs, as pictured on page 82. Describe the conditions of such chain gangs. 3. How can whites and African Americans get along better?

> *VOCABULARY*
> polls, constitutional rights

Convicts building a road
Courtesy, Tampa-Hillsborough County Public Library System

angry whites attacked Perry, lynched him, and left him hanging from a telephone pole.

African Americans were frightened, and many left town as quickly as they could. Most of them had to walk because they did not have cars and there was no railroad. They were scared to talk about what had happened. Many of them wondered if they would ever be treated as Americans.

Further Reading:

Zora Neale Hurston, "The Ocoee Incident," Typescript. Florida Writers Project. P.K. Yonge Library of Florida History, The University of Florida, 1939; *Crisis* 21 (February 1921), p. 170, (March 1921), p. 204; Lester Dabbs, "A Report of the Circumstances and Events of the Race Riot on November 2, 1920, in Ocoee Florida," M.A. Thesis, Stetson University, 1969.

32.

THE ROSEWOOD MASSACRE, JANUARY 1923

A burning cabin in Rosewood, January 4, 1923
Florida State Archives

ROSEWOOD WAS A SMALL African American community on the Gulf Coast of Florida. It was located in Levy County, less than 50 miles from Gainesville. The **population** of Rosewood was only between 150 and 200, but it had its own school and churches. It even had a store, a sugar mill, and a turpentine still. What happened in this small community is an example of the type of justice that African Americans could expect to receive from white Floridians in the early 1920s.

DISCUSSION TOPICS: As you read this chapter, think about the answers to these questions: 1. There is disagreement about how many people were killed in the Rosewood Massacre. How might we try to find out the true number? 2. When something like the Rosewood Massacre takes place, how can a community ever learn to heal itself? 3. How can you help someone get rid of his or her nightmares?

The majority of the African American men who lived there probably worked for the Seaboard Air Line Railroad, in the turpentine industry, or at the Cummer & Sons Cypress Company **sawmill**. Several of the women did laundry for white families. In January 1923 life as African Americans knew it in their peaceful little community came to a violent end.

On New Year's Day in January 1923, a white woman who lived in Sumner, just a few miles from Rosewood, claimed that an African American man had attacked her. African Americans, however, were certain that the white woman's white boyfriend had beaten her. It did not matter. A white woman had accused an African American male of the attack, and a group of white men gathered to

> *VOCABULARY*
> population, sawmill, witnesses

The ruins of a house near Rosewood.
Florida State Archives

find him. They used a hunting dog, which led them to Rosewood.

Even though they were looking for one man, the entire Rosewood community suffered. For a week, whites, who were joined by others from as far away as Georgia and other Florida cities, brought terror to the African American community. They burned the houses, the school, and the churches. White men tortured a man named Sam Carter to make him reveal where the attacker was. They cut off his ears and fingers for souvenirs. Some say that James Carrier, who was paralyzed, was forced to dig his own grave before being shot and killed. Women were not spared either. Ms. Lexie Gordon managed to get her children to safety before she was killed and thrown into a burning house.

African American men, women, and children hid in the woods to escape the violent whites. It was the first week in January and very cold. Many of the people hiding in the woods were in their nightclothes. They were cold and hungry. Many of those who survived thought they were being hunted like rabbits.

Some whites in the area tried to stop the violence and to help the African Americans. One such man was John Wright, who was one of the few whites who lived in Rosewood. John Wright gave ammunition to African Americans to defend themselves. He and his wife rescued many of the women and children who were hiding and helped them to safety. A train owned by two white brothers, John and William Bryce, was sent to rescue the women and children. The train took them to safety.

There are many different accounts of what happened at Rosewood. Several newspapers reported that only seven or eight African Americans were killed. Some **witnesses**, however, claim that the number killed was much higher. As many as 30 or 40 African American men and women may have been killed in the Rosewood Massacre.

Those who survived never returned to Rosewood. They moved to other cities and some even left the state. Some changed their names and never spoke of Rosewood again. They could not, however, ever forget the horrible memories of Rosewood. There are still some African Americans alive who are haunted by those memories.

Further reading:
Gary Moore, "Rosewood," *The Floridian* 25 July 1982, pp. 6-19.

33.

J. R. E. LEE, PRESIDENT OF FLORIDA AGRICULTURAL & MECHANICAL COLLEGE, 1864-1944

J. R. E. Lee
Florida State Archives

WHEN THE FLORIDA BOARD OF CONTROL hired James Robert Edward Lee, Sr., as president of Florida Agricultural and Mechanical College (FAMC) in 1924, they were hopeful that he could restore calm and provide the leadership and skills necessary to move the state college for African Americans forward.

James Robert Edward Lee, Sr., was born a slave in Texas in 1864. His parents knew how important education was so they made sure that he went to school and studied. He graduated from Bishop College in Marshall, Texas, with high honors in 1889.

Lee taught at several schools before coming to FAMC. He worked for Booker T. Washington at Tuskegee Institute in Alabama and also taught school in Texas, South Carolina, and Missouri. When the Florida Board of Control hired him in 1924, he was working for the National Urban League in New York City.

Under President Lee's leadership, FAMC experienced tremendous growth. He raised money from private organizations and per-

DISCUSSION TOPICS: As you read this chapter, think about the answers to these questions: 1. Why is education so important to getting ahead in the world? 2. Why is class size an important part of learning? 3. Why is a band, like the FAMU band which is partly pictured on page 86, not necessary, but still somewhat important for a high school or college or university?

VOCABULARY
administration, campus, diploma

The marching band
Florida State Archives

suaded the state legislature to give more money to the school. New buildings were constructed and existing facilities improved. President Lee hired better-trained teachers and convinced the state legislature to increase their salaries. By reducing class size, improving the library, and increasing the number of college-trained teachers, President Lee raised FAMC's academic standards. In 1935, the Southern Association of Colleges and Secondary Schools gave FAMC an "A" rating.

During President Lee's **administration** FAMC became more involved with the African American community. Teacher-training workshops were held both on and off **campus**. Professors traveled to the various communities to give instruction to those who were working on their high school **diploma** or just trying to improve themselves. Workshops for farmers and ministers were held as well as health clinics. Student enrollment also increased.

Because of President Lee's many im-

provements, the FAMC of 1944 did not resemble the FAMC of 1924. Academically, it was a much better institution. There were better students, teachers, and facilities. More importantly, President Lee had changed the negative "I don't care" attitude that many whites had about FAMC. The governors of Florida as well as the state legislature realized how important FAMC was and gave it more money. President Lee was largely responsible for putting FAMC on the right track to becoming one of country's best schools for African Americans.

Further reading:
Leedell W. Neyland, *Twelve Black Floridians* (Tallahassee: Florida Agricultural and Mechanical University Foundation, 1970); Leedell W. Neyland, *Florida Agricultural and Mechanical University: A Centennial History 1887-1987* (Tallahassee: The Florida A & M University Foundation, 1987).

34.
BLANCHE ARMWOOD, EDUCATOR, ADMINISTRATOR, RACE LEADER, 1890-1939

Blanche Armwood (Beatty) with members of the Tampa Urban League, May 1925
Courtesy, Tampa-Hillsborough County Public Library System

BLANCHE ARMWOOD WAS BORN in Tampa, Florida, on January 23, 1890. Her father, Levin Armwood, Jr., was an important man in the community. At various times he was a deputy sheriff, supervisor of county roads, and Tampa's first African American police officer. It was unusual for women or for African Americans to hold these positions during this period. Blanche lived in a middle-class family, and her home was filled with books and music. Her parents taught her and her four older brothers and sisters right from wrong and the value of hard work.

The church and school played a major role in Blanche's life. She sang in the church choir and attended the best school in the city for African American students, Saint Peter Claver Catholic School. Both the church and

DISCUSSION TOPICS: As you read this chapter, think about the answers to these questions: 1. What is the value of having books and music in a home with children? 2. Look at the photograph of the woman washing clothes; how could Blanche Armwood have helped her? 3. Compare the students in the photo on page 89 with students of today, for example in terms of clothes.

> *VOCABULARY*
> thrifty, self-reliant, accredited, Bethune-Cookman College

Washday in Miami
Florida State Archives

the school helped to develop Blanche's leadership skills and her great speaking ability. She graduated from St. Peter Claver with very good grades. There was no high school for Blanche to attend in Tampa, so she went to Atlanta, Georgia, to attend Spelman College.

After graduating from Spelman, Ms. Armwood returned to Tampa and began teaching in the local schools. She was a teacher for seven years. In 1913, Ms. Armwood quit her teaching job and began setting up schools of household arts for African American girls and women. She taught them how to work with their hands and how to be **thrifty** and **self-reliant**.

In 1922, Ms. Armwood was appointed Supervisor of Negro Schools for Tampa and Hillsborough County, a position she held until 1930. She accomplished a lot in this position. Education for African Americans and whites was not equal during that time.

For example, white children attended school for nine months, while African American children attended for only six months. Ms. Armwood worked hard to change this. By 1926, African American students were attending school for nine months, too.

After African American students finished the eighth grade, their education was considered complete. There was no high school for them to attend. But under Ms. Armwood's leadership, Booker T. Washington High School, the first **accredited** school for African Americans in Hillsborough County, was established.

Ms. Armwood was also a leader in humanitarian efforts and race relations. In 1922, she became the executive secretary of the Tampa Urban League, an organization that worked to improve the condition of African Americans. The Urban League established a day-care center, a kindergarten, and

Dunbar High School

health-care programs for African Americans.

Blanche Armwood was a very good friend of Mary McLeod Bethune and helped to raise money for Ms. Bethune's school, **Bethune-Cookman College**, in Daytona Beach. The two women also belonged to many of the same clubs. Ms. Armwood was very active in both the National Association for the Advancement of Colored People and also the National Association of Colored Women. Like Ms. Bethune, Ms. Armwood condemned lynching and discrimination against African Americans. She was a member of the Republican Party and often during an election year traveled around the country encouraging African Americans to vote for Republicans seeking political office.

Ms. Armwood decided in 1934 that she wanted to become a lawyer. She enrolled in Howard Law School in Washington, D.C., the nation's capital. When she graduated in 1938, she became the first African American woman from Florida to graduate from an accredited law school. Ms. Armwood dreamed of becoming a judge but died in 1939.

Often called a "female Booker T. Washington," Blanche Armwood worked hard to improve the lives of African Americans in Florida. She had a great impact on education for African Americans in Tampa and Hillsborough County. Her courage in denouncing racism and lynching was admirable. The Blanche Armwood Comprehensive High School, named in her honor, opened in 1984 and was dedicated in February 1985.

Further reading:

Mary Burke, "The Success of Blanche Armwood," *The Sunland Tribune* 13 (November 1987), pp. 38-43; John R. Durham, "Blanche Armwood: The Early Years 1890-1922," M.A. Thesis, University of South Florida, 1988; Lottie Montgomery Clark, "Negro Women Leaders of Florida," M.A. Thesis, The Florida State University, 1947.

35.

RAY CHARLES, SINGER, ENTERTAINER, 1930-

Ray Charles
Florida State Archives

RAY CHARLES IS A WONDERFUL EXAMPLE of an African American overcoming **obstacles** to reach the top. He is one of Florida's most successful and well-known entertainers. Even though he was born in Albany, Georgia, Ray Charles Robinson moved to Greenville, Florida, just a few months after his birth in 1930.

DISCUSSION TOPICS: As you read this chapter, think about the answers to these questions: 1. If you were going blind, what would you do? 2. How can we make the life of blind people easier? 3. Compare the photographs of the two groups of children playing musical instruments and singing. Compare the groups in terms of age and instruments.

His family was very poor and moved around a lot. There was generally no indoor plumbing in the houses he lived in; people used **outhouses** instead. His father was not around much, but his mother washed and ironed clothes for whites. She was a strong **disciplinarian**. She taught him not to beg and not to steal. In spite of the poverty, Ray Charles was a happy little boy.

From the time he was three years old, Ray Charles loved music. He claims that music was born in him. He wrote in his

> *VOCABULARY*
> obstacles, outhouse, disciplinarian,
> braille, trio

90

autobiography that "Music was one of my parts. Like my ribs, my liver, my kidneys, my heart. Like my blood. It was a force already within me when I arrived on the scene. It was a necessity for me like food or water. And from the moment I learned that there were piano keys to be mashed, I started mashing 'em, trying to make sounds out of feelings" (*Brother Ray*, p. 8).

When he was five years old, Ray Charles began to have trouble with his eyes. Two years later, he was completely blind.

His mother insisted that, in spite of his blindness, he should be able to take care of himself. So Ray Charles learned to wash and dress himself, to do household chores, and to play outside. He even rode his bicycle.

At age seven Ray Charles left Greenville to attend the State School for the Deaf and the Blind in St. Augustine. He was homesick. It was the first time that he had ever been away from home, and he missed his mother and his friends. He cried a lot, but eventually he adjusted. At this school Ray Charles learned **braille**, which enabled him to read with his fingers. Ray Charles also began his formal music lessons at school. He practiced on the piano and the clarinet.

After his mother died in 1945, Ray Charles left school. He was only fifteen years old, but felt that he could make his own way, hopefully in the field of music. He moved to Jacksonville where he found jobs playing the piano in various halls and clubs, before moving on to Orlando and Tampa. He admired African American musicians and singers Nat "King" Cole and Charles Brown and imitated their style. Eventually, Ray Charles would develop a style all his own.

Ray Charles struggled for many years.

"Juvenile band" at Fernandina 1878
Florida State Archives

Times were hard and jobs were scarce. Sometimes he went for days without food, but he never gave up. Music was his life, and he wanted to use it to make a better life for himself. Things improved after he moved to Seattle, Washington, around 1948 and got a job in a nightclub. He organized a **trio**, and before long Ray Charles and his trio were being heard on the radio. He recorded his first song in 1948 and soon had a hit record.

Hit record followed hit record, and by the 1950's Ray Charles was a star. Songs such as "I Got A Woman, "A Fool For You," "Drown in My Own Tears," "Hallelujah," "I Love Her So," and "Georgia On My Mind" are just a few of Ray Charles's big hits.

It did not matter that Ray Charles was born poor, lived in a segregated society, or that he could not see; he followed his dream. Music was important to him, and he perfected his skill. He played the piano, the clarinet, and the saxophone. He also learned to play more than one type of music. He could play jazz and the blues and also Beethoven and Chopin and even country music. In addition, he wrote and arranged music. He did it all.

Ray Charles did not let his handicaps keep him from making his dream come true. It was not easy and it did not happen overnight, but his dream came true. He has brought much joy to music lovers all around the world–both African American and white. Florida recognized Ray Charles's musical talents and accomplishments when it inducted him into the Florida Hall of Fame in 1992.

Further reading:
Ray Charles and David Ritz, *Brother Ray: Ray Charles' Own Story* (New York: Dial Press, 1978).

Young musicians
Florida State Archives

36.
TEACHERS' SALARY EQUALIZATION CASES

A rural Duval County school for African Americans
Florida State Archives

AFRICAN AMERICAN TEACHERS, principals, and administrators in Florida were discriminated against in the amount of salary they received. In 1930, the average monthly **salary** for white males was $169.20, for African American males $84.20, for white females $115.80, and for African American females $61.60. The differences in salaries for African American and white teachers continued. The average annual salary for white teachers continued to be much more than the average annual salary for African Americans.

DISCUSSION TOPICS: As you read this chapter, think about the answers to these questions: 1. Why is it better for people to file suit in court rather than have a fistfight when they feel they have been hurt? 2. How do you think salaries of people like teachers, lawyers, and doctors are set? 3. Describe the two photographs of the adult learners in school.

Various organizations and individuals condemned the low **wage** that African American teachers received. During the 1940s African American educators in Escambia, Brevard, Duval, Hillsborough, and Palm Beach counties went to the state courts to fight for better salaries. Vernon McDaniel, the principal of Washington High School in Pensacola, filed a **suit** against the Escambia County School Board in 1941. He asked that those who have equal work and **qualifications** earn the same salary, not only for himself, but for all teachers who were being discriminated against. Even though white teachers

---

VOCABULARY
salary, wage, suit, qualifications

Washington School in Pensacola, adult education class, June 17, 1935
Florida State Archives

were opposed, the Escambia County School Board agreed to make the salaries equal.

Many other African American teachers around the state also filed suit against school boards to try to get equal pay for themselves. Oftentimes African American teachers lost their jobs when they went to court to try to increase their salary. They all received support from the Florida State Teachers Association (FSTA).

The FSTA was an organization of African American teachers who gave each other support and tried to improve the quality of education for African American students in Florida. While not all of the teacher equalization suits were successful and the results were not always immediate, some progress was made in bringing the salaries of African American teachers closer to those of white teachers.

Further reading:
Gilbert Porter and Leedell W. Neyland, *History of the Florida State Teachers Association* (Washington, DC: National Education Association, 1977).

37.

STRAWBERRY SCHOOLS

Returning from the strawberry fields
P.K. Yonge Library of Florida History, University of Florida

IN MANY AREAS IN FLORIDA, African American students attended school for only a few months. The school term was often planned to help area farmers. For example, in Hillsborough County, students went to **"strawberry schools,"** that is, they went to school during the summer and picked strawberries in the winter and spring. In Baker and Duval counties, students ten years old and above left school to pick vegetables.

When farmers in St. Johns County needed help to **harvest** their potato crop, the schools were closed and the students went to work in the fields. The same thing happened in, Jackson County, where there were a lot of tobacco farms. White students attended school for up to nine months in most counties, but African American students sometimes received as little as three months of schooling. Some counties tried to make up the difference by opening schools during the summer.

DISCUSSION TOPICS: As you read this chapter, think about the answers to these questions: 1. Look at the photograph of the four children returning from the strawberry fields. How can you describe them? 2. Look at the photograph of the children near the ox teams. Do you think those children attended school regularly? If not, what jobs might they have had around their homes? 3. What are the arguments for and against keeping schools open the whole year?

VOCABULARY
strawberry schools, harvest, reforms

Barberville School
Florida State Archives

In Broward County during the 1930s and 1940s, students went to school from August to December and worked picking beans and other vegetables from January to May. Farmers did not have to pay children as much as adults, but poor families needed the extra income earned by their children.

African Americans in Marion County hired a lawyer in 1932 and forced the school board to reopen African American schools that it had closed. In 1943, the Broward County School Board closed African American schools so that students could help harvest crops. The students' parents and teachers complained that white schools were not closed and forced the school board to keep African American schools open for nine months. By the 1950s **reforms** were being made in education, and the practice of closing school so that children could pick fruit and vegetables came to an end.

Ox teams & homes
Florida State Archives

Further reading:

J. Irving Scott, *The Education of Black People in Florida* (Philadelphia: Dorrance & Company, 1974); Milly St. Julien and Gary R. Mormino, "Women in Florida History" (Produced and distributed for the National Resource Center for Middle Grades Educa-tion and the College of Education, the University of South Florida, 1987); Martin Richardson, "What the Florida Negro Does." Typescript. Florida Writers Project, P.K. Yonge Library of Florida History, The University of Florida, 1937.

38.
ALONZO S. "JAKE" GAITHER, FOOTBALL COACH, 1903-

Jake Gaither
Florida State Archives

DURING THE 1950s JAKE GAITHER and the Florida Agricultural and Mechanical University (FAMU) football team seemed to **dominate** African American college football. Jake Gaither and his FAMU teams won the National Negro Collegiate Football Championship in 1950, 1954, 1957, 1959, and 1961.

DISCUSSION TOPICS: As you read this chapter, think about the answers to these questions: 1. What can athletes learn in sports like basketball, baseball, and football that will help them in life? 2. The nickname of FAMU's athletic team is the Rattlers; what does that word mean? 3. Because most athletes do not become professional athletes, how should they prepare themselves for non athletic careers?

Alonzo S. "Jake" Gaither was born in Tennessee, but was raised in a small mining town in Kentucky. His family was poor and everybody had to work. Jake found a job after school shining shoes. His father was a minister, and many people expected Jake to become a minister too. After he finished the eighth grade, Jake went to Knoxville College in Tennessee, where he completed high school and college. While at Knoxville College, Jake played football. He liked the sport

> *VOCABULARY*
> dominate, debate, seminary, brain tumor, role model

97

a lot, but even though he played for six years, he scored only one touchdown. He was also on the school **debate** team which won many college debates with other schools. Jake majored in social and political science and planned to attend a **seminary** to prepare to become a minister after graduating from Knoxville College.

His father's death changed his plans. Jake had to put off going to the seminary to take care of his mother and his three brothers and sisters. Luckily, he found a coaching job at a high school in North Carolina, where he stayed for eight years and learned much about coaching before moving on to a community college in Virginia.

In Virginia his reputation as a coach began to grow, and he soon was offered and accepted a job as an assistant coach at Florida Agricultural and Mechanical University in Tallahassee. In 1942, he coached the FAMU basketball team to a conference championship. Later that year, however, tragedy struck when Jake almost died from a **brain tumor.**

Fortunately, he survived an operation to remove the tumor, but his recovery was slow. He had to walk with a cane and had difficulty keeping his balance. Jake was disappointed when FAMU's President, J. R. E. Lee, told him that he could not return to coaching, but Jake loved coaching and was determined to change Lee's mind. An opportunity to return to coaching came in 1944 when President Lee died and head coach William Bell went into the Army. Jake Gaither was appointed acting Director of Athletics and Physical Education, and he became the temporary head football coach. Coach Bell decided not to return to FAMU after he left the military, and Jake became FAMU's permanent head coach.

Jake Gaither hired excellent coaches and recruited gifted athletes such as Bob Hayes. Between 1945 and 1969, Gaither's football teams won 203 games and lost only 34. FAMU won the Southern Inter-Collegiate Athletic Conference Championship 23 out of 24 years. He coached undefeated teams in 1957, 1959, and 1961. The National Negro Collegiate Football Championship practically belonged to FAMU.

In his role as coach, Jake Gaither persuaded professional football scouts to take a look at African American football players from small schools. He opened the door for FAMU player Willie Galimore and many others to play professional football. Jake Gaither has received many honors as a coach. In 1961, he was named to the National Intercollegiate Athletic Association's Hall of Fame and in 1962 was named "Small-College Coach of the Year" by the American Football Coaches Association.

But Jake Gaither was more than a coach. He was a **role model** and a teacher to African American youth. He encouraged young men to do their best not only on the football field and basketball court, but in everything they tried to do. For the influence that he has had on young people, the Jake Gaither Recreation Center in Tallahassee, Florida, was named in his honor in 1955. And Gaither Gymnasium on the campus of FAMU is the home of the Rattlers basketball teams. For more about Willie Galimore see #110 on the Florida Black Heritage Trail: St. Augustine's Willie Galimore Community Center (p. 170).

Further reading:
Wyatt Blassingame, *Jake Gaither, Winning Coach* (Champaign, IL: Garrard Publishing Company, 1969); Leedell W. Neyland, *Twelve Black Floridians* (Tallahassee: Florida Agricultural and Mechanical University Foundation, 1970); Leedell W. Neyland, *Florida Agricultural and Mechanical University: A Centennial History, 1887-1987* (Tallahassee: The Florida A & M University Foundation, 1987).

39.
ROBERT LEE "BOB" HAYES, WORLD'S FASTEST HUMAN, 1942-

Florida State Archives

ROBERT HAYES EARNED HIS REPUTATION as the "World's Fastest Human" in 1963 at the National AAU (Amateur Athletic Union of the United States) Championship Meet, where he established a world record in the 100-yard dash. He was clocked at the amazing speed of 9.1 seconds.

Robert was born in Jacksonville in 1942. His father was a **disabled** war veteran, and his mother worked as a maid. Unfortunately, his parents separated, and Robert

DISCUSSION TOPICS: As you read this chapter, think about the answers to these questions: 1. If most of the world uses the metric system of measurements, should the United States choose the metric system also? 2. What are the main events in track meets? Which are the most difficult? 3. How do runners in a relay run the race?

> *VOCABULARY*
> disabled, track meets, sopho-
> more

Bob Hayes weighs in at the Tallahassee
airport on his way to the Olympic trials
Florida State Archives

lived with various relatives. As a teenager he worked as a shoe-shine boy to earn money.

Bob was an amazing athlete; even as a youngster, he liked to run, and he easily outran his playmates. In high school he attracted the attention of the track coach, who taught him how to run fast and win **track meets**. When Bob graduated from high school, he could run the 100-yard dash in 9.6 seconds, but he knew he could do even better.

Bob enjoyed running track, but football was his favorite sport. In 1960, he won a scholarship to Florida Agricultural and Mechanical University in Tallahassee, Florida, where he played football for the famous coach Jake Gaither. As a **sophomore** Bob averaged an amazing 10.7 yards every time he carried the football. He thrilled his fans both on the field and on the track.

Bob Hayes was the first African American to play in the Senior Bowl football game held every year in Mobile, Alabama; in that game he was named the South's most valuable player. In December 1964, he signed a professional football contract with the Dallas Cowboys. Later he made the National Football League's All Rookie Professional Team and played in the All Pro Bowl.

Bob Hayes probably attracted more attention as a track star than he did as a football star. At the 1964 Olympics held in Tokyo, Japan, he tied both the world and Olympic records in the 100-meter race with his 10.0 second time. He also ran on the U.S. 400-meter relay team which won a gold medal and set new world and Olympic records.

After playing football and running track, Bob went on to become a successful businessman. He has been a good role model for thousands of African American youth who want to combine hard work in school and hard work on the athletic field.

Further reading:
Leedell W. Neyland, *Twelve Black Floridians* (Tallahassee: Florida Agricultural and Mechanical University Foundation, 1970); *Florida Magazine* October 31, 1964.

40.
S. D. McGILL, CIVIL RIGHTS ATTORNEY

Eartha M. M. White Collection, Thomas G.
Carpenter Library, University of North Florida

IN 1942, AFRICAN AMERICAN ATTORNEY S. D. MCGILL won the freedom of four men who had spent nine years on **death row**. With the 1940 decision handed down by the United States Supreme Court in *Chambers v. Florida*, Izell Chambers, Charlie Davis, Walter Woodward, and Jack Williamson were granted a new **trial**. The court's decision was celebrated as "a second **Emancipation**."

Simuel Decatur McGill was born in Quincy, Florida, in 1878. While growing up in Sanford, Florida, he dreamed of becoming a lawyer one day. He attended Edward Waters College in Jacksonville and worked part-time as a clerk in the law offices of James Weldon Johnson and J. Douglas Wetmore.

After graduating from Edward Waters College in 1902, S. D., as he preferred to be called, became the only African American

DISCUSSION TOPICS: As you read this chapter, think about the answers to these questions: 1. The death penalty is one of the most controversial issues in the world today. What are the arguments for and against the death penalty? 2. When are some times in people's lives when they use a lawyer?

VOCABULARY
death row, trial, Emancipation,
electrocution, tenant farmers, warrant

student enrolled at Dummer Academy in South Byfield, Massachusetts. He studied hard and did well; for example, he won first place in a speaking contest. While he was at school, Mr. Wetmore wrote him a letter advising him to "knuckle down" and study hard and not waste his time "fooling with the girls."

The students who went to Dummer Academy were often expected to continue their education at Harvard University in Cambridge, Massachusetts. S. D. followed many of his classmates by enrolling at Harvard; he later completed his legal training at Boston University in 1907, was admitted to the Florida Bar in 1908, and opened a law office in Jacksonville, Florida.

Attorney McGill served as lawyer for several African American organizations and businesses. He also represented African Americans in civil rights cases and was an attorney for the National Association for the Advancement of Colored People (NAACP).

He gained a national reputation for his skillful handling of the *Washington vs. State of Florida* case. That case involved Abe Washington, an African American convicted of murder and sentenced to death by hanging in 1923. In 1924, the Florida Legislature abolished death by hanging and replaced it with **electrocution**. Attorney McGill successfully argued before the Florida Supreme Court that the death-by-hanging law was no longer valid and that death by electrocution did not apply to Washington.

As an attorney for the NAACP, S. D. McGill worked nine years on another case that reached the U.S. Supreme Court. The case involved four young African American men: Izell Chambers, Charlie Davis, Walter Woodward, and Jack Williamson, all uneducated **tenant farmers** living in Broward County who were accused of robbing and murdering a white man in Pompano Beach in 1933.

Known as the "Pompano Boys," these four young men were arrested without a **warrant** and, although never formally charged with having committed a crime, were held for five days and nights. They were not allowed to contact their family or friends or even an attorney. The "Pompano Boys" were tortured and forced to confess to a crime they had not committed.

Chambers, Davis, Woodward, and Williamson were found guilty and sentenced to death. In an effort to reverse the guilty verdict, Attorney McGill argued and won a reversal five different times. But in March 1939 the Florida Supreme Court upheld the guilty verdict and the death sentences of the lower court. McGill and the NAACP made an appeal before the United States Supreme Court on January 4, 1940.

On February 12, Abraham Lincoln's birthday, the U.S. Supreme Court reversed the decision of the Florida Supreme Court. Reading the court's unanimous opinion given in *Chambers v. Florida*, Justice Black said that "the very circumstances surrounding their confinement and their questioning without any formal charges having been brought, were such as to fill petitioners with terror and frightful misgivings."

Since the Pompano Boys' civil rights had been violated, they were entitled to a new trial. With attorney McGill successfully arguing their case, they were found not guilty and finally released from prison in March 1942.

Attorney McGill could have given up, but he did not. For nine long years he pursued justice for the poor men who had been unjustly arrested and charged with murder. African Americans all across the country were happy for the Pompano Boys and proud of S. D. McGill.

Further reading:
Crisis 47 (March 1940), pp. 81, 85; (June 1940), pp. 190, 206-207.

41.
VIRGIL D. HAWKINS, 1906-1988

The Ku Klux Klan marching in Miami in 1925
Florida State Archives

WHEN VIRGIL D. HAWKINS was only eight years old, he decided that he wanted to become a lawyer someday. One day he went to the courthouse with his father and witnessed a judge sentencing several African American men to six months in jail for gambling. He thought that the judge had been unfair and decided then that he would become a lawyer to help such men. When he was 13 years old, his dream of becoming a lawyer was strengthened when his cousin was lynched by whites.

Virgil Hawkins was born in 1906 in Okahumpka, Florida. He graduated from high school in Jacksonville and attended Lincoln University in Pennsylvania. He began to save money for law school by selling insurance and later becoming a school teacher. Virgil Hawkins was 42 years old by the time he had enough money to go to law school. Since there was no law school for African Americans in Florida, he applied in 1949 for admission to the University of Florida Law School in Gainesville.

DISCUSSION TOPICS: As you read this chapter, think about the answers to these questions: 1. Why do you think Virgil Hawkins kept trying to enter law school? 2. Does anyone in the class know any lawyers? What do those lawyers specialize in? 3. Look at the photograph of the Ku Klux Klan in Miami. Can you describe what is going on?

VOCABULARY
suit, tuition, appeal, unaccredited

It was against Florida law for African Americans and whites to attend school together, and the Board of Control decided not to allow Mr. Hawkins to attend the University of Florida Law School. Since he met all of the other qualifications, he was denied admission simply because of the color of his skin. Mr. Hawkins decided to take his case to court and filed **suit** in the state Supreme Court. He wanted the court to force the state to admit him to law school.

The state put up a strong fight. It offered to pay Mr. Hawkins's **tuition** if he attended school out of state, but he refused. He did not understand why he should have to leave his home state just to be able to attend law school. It was unfair. Whites who wanted to become lawyers did not have to leave the state.

To make sure that other African Americans did not sue them, the Board of Control agreed to open a law school for African Americans at the Florida Agricultural and Mechanical College (FAMC) for Negroes in Tallahassee.

Virgil Hawkins could temporarily take courses at the University of Florida until the law school at FAMC was ready. The Supreme Court was impressed with the solution offered by the state of Florida and the Board of Control.

But Mr. Hawkins was not admitted to the University of Florida Law School, even on a temporary basis. He asked the state Supreme Court for help again and again. In 1952, the Florida Supreme Court dismissed his case, arguing that he could attend the law school at FAMC. Mr. Hawkins then went to the United States Supreme Court for help. In 1956, the U.S. Supreme Court, the highest court in the land, ordered the state of Florida to admit Virgil Hawkins to the University of Florida Law School without further delay.

But he still was not admitted. The state of Florida disobeyed an order from the U.S. Supreme Court and claimed that violence would result if Mr. Hawkins were admitted to the Gainesville law school. The U.S. Supreme Court refused to hear another

University of Florida, Gainesville, 1948
Florida State Archives

104

appeal from Mr. Hawkins, but in 1958 a federal district court judge ordered the University of Florida graduate schools opened to all qualified African Americans. This was a significant victory. But not for Virgil Darnell Hawkins! The University of Florida now claimed that he did not meet its admissions standards.

Mr. Hawkins, of course, was very disappointed. After nine years of asking the courts for help, he had waited long enough to make his life-long dream of becoming a lawyer a reality. Virgil Hawkins entered the **unaccredited** New England School of Law in Boston, Massachusetts, and graduated in 1964. He returned to Florida eager to help the poor and disadvantaged.

But his battles were not over. According to Florida law, graduates from unaccredited law schools could not take the state's bar examination. That meant that Virgil Hawkins could not practice law in Florida. Instead he worked as an insurance salesman, a teacher, a public relations director, and served as director of a community action agency. He still hoped to practice law.

At age 69, Virgil Hawkins tried once again to fulfill his dream. In 1975, he asked the Florida Supreme Court to be admitted to the Florida Bar. In 1976, the court allowed Mr. Hawkins to become a lawyer without taking the bar examination. After studying the law some more and working with a practicing attorney, Virgil Hawkins finally opened a law office in Leesburg. His dream had finally come true. The 70-year-old Hawkins had spent almost 30 years fighting a system designed to keep him on the bottom. Even though racism and discrimination denied him the same opportunities that whites had, Virgil Hawkins never gave up. He continued to fight not only for his rights as an American but for the rights of all.

Virgil Hawkins's strength and courage are an inspiration to all. The state university system's Virgil D. Hawkins Scholarship for minority students in law school honors him and serves as a reminder of his long struggle and ultimate victory.

Further reading:
Algia R. Cooper, "Brown V. Board of Education and Virgil Darnell Hawkins Twenty-Eight Years and Six Petitions to Justice," *The Journal of Negro History* 64 (Winter 1979), pp. 1+; *Tallahassee Democrat* July 28, 1978, May 11, 1984.

42.

HARRY T. MOORE,
EDUCATOR AND CIVIL RIGHTS LEADER,
1905-1951

Ku Klux Klan, Tallahassee, Florida
Florida State Archives

HARRY TYSON MOORE was born in Houston, Florida, a small community outside of Live Oak in Suwannee County, in November 1905. He was nicknamed "Doc" because he was an excellent student who liked such subjects as math and science. "Doc" graduated from Florida Memorial College in 1925. Twenty-six years later he earned a college degree from Bethune-Cookman College in Daytona Beach. Mr. Moore became a teacher in several different Florida cities, including Houston, Titusville, Cocoa, and Mims.

Even though he was a shy, quiet, and **scholarly** man, Harry Moore disliked injustice of any kind. It concerned him that white teachers made more money than African American teachers, that African Americans were not allowed to vote, and that they were often beaten and killed by whites and the Ku Klux Klan.

In 1934, Harry Moore organized a branch of the National Association for the

DISCUSSION TOPICS: As you read this chapter, think about the answers to these questions: 1. What are nicknames? Does anyone in class have one that they are willing to share with the class? What do the nicknames mean? 2. Can you name any other martyrs you have heard or read about?

Advancement of Colored People (NAACP) in Brevard County, Florida, to help right some of the wrongs committed against African Americans. From 1941 to 1946 Mr. Moore served as president of the state conference of the NAACP and in 1946 became its executive secretary.

As an officer of the NAACP, Mr. Moore led the struggle to achieve equal rights for African Americans. He also led the effort to equalize teacher salaries. John E. Gilbert, a friend of Moore's, filed the first suit for equal teachers' pay in 1937. This was the first of several such cases. Often when African American teachers took their cases to court, they were fired from their teaching positions. Mr. Moore lost his teaching job, as well.

Harry Moore also fought for the right of African Americans to vote. If African Americans were not allowed to vote, he asked, how could they improve their situation? Through the NAACP and the Progressive Voters League, which he helped to organize, Mr. Moore encouraged African Americans to fight for their rights. He encouraged them, in spite of the consequences, to register and then to exercise their right to vote. When African Americans were denied this opportunity, Mr. Moore advised them to file discrimination suits. The NAACP helped African Americans who did so.

Harry Moore was very outspoken about white violence against African Americans. He pointed out that African Americans were beaten for moving into white neighborhoods, for trying to vote, and for violating **Jim Crow laws**. The Ku Klux Klan often burned crosses to frighten African Americans. Sometimes mobs arrested and killed African Americans

before a trial could take place. Harry Moore tried to stop this. He bitterly protested the lynching of Jesse James Payne in Madison, Florida, and the mob violence that followed the arrest of four African American men in Groveland, Florida. He complained to the governor.

When Sheriff W. V. McCall shot one and killed another of the men arrested in the Groveland case, Mr. Moore was angry. He worked hard to show the world how African Americans were treated in Florida and to make sure that Sheriff McCall was fired and arrested. He did not give up, but he was to pay a heavy price for his devotion to securing rights for his people.

On Christmas night, 1951, Harry T. Moore and his wife, Harriett, were killed when three pounds of dynamite exploded under their bedroom. Although it was never proven, many believed that the Ku Klux Klan was responsible for planting that dynamite. Harry Moore was a freedom fighter and the first NAACP official to die in the line of duty. He risked his life to make life better for African Americans in Florida, and for that he became a **martyr** and a symbol to African Americans around the country who continued in the struggle to make the United States equal for all. For more about this great man see #11 in the Florida Black Heritage Trail in this book: the Harry T. Moore Center in Cocoa.

Further reading:

Caroline Emmons Poore, "Striking the First Blow: Harry T. Moore and the Fight for Black Equality in Florida," M.A. Thesis, The Florida State University, 1992; Gloster B. Current, "Martyr for a Cause," *Crisis* 59 (February 1952), pp. 72-81, 133-134; Leedell W. Neyland, *Twelve Black Floridians* (Tallahassee: Florida Agricultural and Mechanical University Foundation, 1970).

43.

REVEREND C. K. STEELE, CIVIL RIGHTS LEADER, 1914-1980

Rev. C. K. Steele
Florida State Archives

AFRICAN AMERICAN MINISTERS and the church played a major part in the civil rights movement in the United States. In Tallahassee, Florida, the Reverend Charles Kenzie Steele provided the leadership that brought about change for thousands of African Americans.

Charles Kenzie Steele was born in Gary, West Virginia, in 1914. His father worked as a **coal miner**, which was a very

dangerous job, but it paid well. Charles grew up as an only child in a good home environment. Even though Gary, West Virginia, was in the South, **race relations** in Charles's hometown were pretty good. African Americans were not forced to ride in the back of the bus, they participated in politics as voters, and they received equal pay for equal work.

Charles knew when he was very young that he wanted to be a minister. His grandmother and his mother encouraged him. After graduating from high school in 1934, Charles went to Atlanta, Georgia, to attend

---

DISCUSSION TOPICS: As you read this chapter, think about the answers to these questions: 1. Why is a boycott often very successful? 2. Look at the photograph of Reverend C. K. Steele in front of his church. What can you tell about him and his church from the photograph? 3. Look at the photograph of a revival. How does a religious service in a revival tent differ from a religious service in a church like the one that Reverend C. K. Steele preached in?

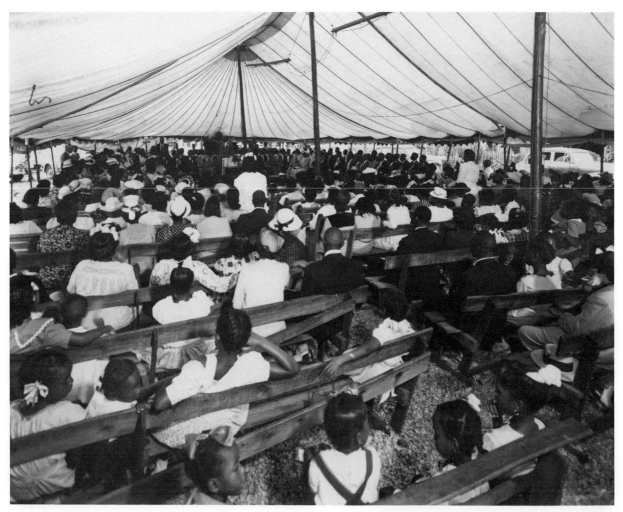

People attending a revival meeting in Tampa
Courtesy, Tampa-Hillsborough County Public Library System

Morehouse College, a school which helped to prepare him for his role as a leader. At the end of his first year at Morehouse, Steele was ordained as a minister. It was a dream come true for him, and he spent the summer preaching in churches in his hometown. After he graduated from Morehouse in 1938, the Hall Street Baptist Church in Montgomery, Alabama, hired him as their minister.

The Reverend Steele was pastor at the Alabama church until 1945, when he became minister of the Springfield Baptist Church in Augusta, Georgia. In 1951, he moved with his wife and children to Tallahassee, Florida, to serve the Bethel Baptist Church.

There in Tallahassee, Reverend Steele gained a reputation as a civil rights leader. He became local president of the National Asso-

ciation for the Advancement of Colored People (NAACP) and president of the Inter-Civic Council. He was a good friend of Dr. Martin Luther King, Jr., and, like King, believed in nonviolent protest. He was also a charter member and first vice-president of the Southern Christian Leadership Conference (SCLC).

In 1956, Florida Agricultural and Mechanical University (FAMU) students led a **boycott** against the local bus company. They wanted to bring an end to a system that required African Americans to sit at the back of the bus. If all the seats at the back of the bus were taken, African Americans had to stand, even if there were empty seats up front in the white section. Sometimes, African American passengers had to give their seats to whites if all of the seats in the white section were taken.

109

Reverend Steele helped to organize the bus boycott and was largely responsible for keeping it nonviolent, although he received many threats from whites. The Ku Klux Klan marched past his house and threw bricks through his windows, all of which made him fear for his family's safety.

During the bus boycott, which lasted for more than a year, Reverend Steele provided moral as well as spiritual leadership. He participated in **voter registration** drives and lectured around the country to raise money for the movement. By May 1958, the buses in Tallahassee were completely desegregated.

Even though African Americans could sit anywhere they wanted to on the buses, Reverend Steele knew that the battle for complete **equality** was just beginning. He considered it his "moral obligation" to continue his protest against **injustice**. He condemned separate schools and segregated hotels, restaurants, and movie theaters. He wanted African Americans to be able to vote and to run for political office. At great personal sacrifice, the Reverend Charles Kenzie Steele fought segregation and racism as the leader of the civil rights movement in Tallahassee.

Further reading:

Gregory B. Padgett, "C. K. Steele and the Tallahassee Bus Boycott," M.A. Thesis, The Florida State University, 1977.

44.
THE TALLAHASSEE BUS BOYCOTT, 1956

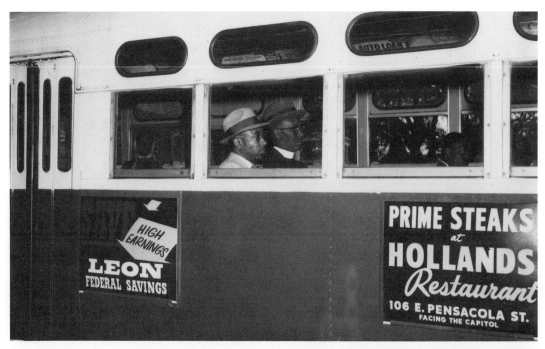

Rev. C. K. Steele during the bus boycott
Florida State Archives

ON MAY 27, 1956, CARRIE PATTERSON AND WILHEMINA JAKES waited for a bus to take them to their home on West Jennings Street in Tallahassee, Florida. They were students at Florida Agricultural and Mechanical University (FAMU). When the bus arrived, Carrie and Wilhemina got on. It was crowded and almost full. They paid their **fare** and looked for a place to sit. They were tired and could not wait to sit down. The two girls took the only two seats available. The two empty seats, however, were in the "white" section of the bus.

When the bus driver ordered them to leave their seats and to stand in the "colored" section of the bus, they refused. Carrie and Wilhemina offered to leave the bus if their fares were returned, but the bus driver would not give them their money back. Instead, he called the police.

The police arrested Carrie and Wilhemina and charged them with "inciting a riot." They were released from jail on $25 **bond** and later had the **charges** against them dropped, but the incident would not die. That night, whites who were angry that the girls had disobeyed one of segregation's rules burned a cross in front of their home.

FAMU students were sick and tired of the way that bus drivers treated African

DISCUSSION TOPICS: As you read this chapter, think about the answers to these questions: 1. Why is the policy of "first come, first served" a good one? What does it mean? 2. Why does it help to have many people join together to make a boycott effective? 3. Look at the photograph of the Tallahassee demonstrations from the early 1960s. Describe the scene.

> *VOCABULARY*
> fare, bond, charges, nonviolent,
> car pools, barriers

Florida A&M students protest the arrest of 23 of their classmates
Florida State Archives

Americans and decided to support Carrie and Wilhemina. Hundreds of African Americans at FAMU and in the community agreed to boycott (not use) city buses.

FAMU students began the bus boycott, but African American ministers and community leaders soon took over. An Inter-Civic Council (ICC) was organized with the Reverend C. K. Steele as president. The purpose of the ICC was to bring an end to segregated seating on Tallahassee's buses. It adopted a **nonviolent** position.

Reverend Steele and the ICC asked the bus company to adopt a first-come, first-served seating policy, that white bus drivers be polite to their African American customers, and that African American bus drivers be hired to drive the buses that went through the African American community. The boycott was to continue until these conditions were met.

African Americans supported the bus boycott and formed **car pools** to take people to and from work. Tallahassee whites were angry and tried to bring an end to the boycott. The police arrested Reverend Steele and many car pool drivers, but African Americans continued to find other ways to get to work. The boycott was so successful that the

bus company lost money and was forced to close for a month.

"We would rather walk in dignity than ride in humiliation" became the slogan for the Tallahassee bus boycott. The bus company did finally agree to hire African American bus drivers for routes in the African American community; some African Americans rode those routes only. The bus boycott celebrated its first anniversary in May 1957. By May 1958 the boycott succeeded when the policy for seating on Tallahassee buses was changed to first-come, first-served. African Americans no longer had to sit in the back of the bus, but could sit wherever they wanted.

The success of the Tallahassee bus boycott urged African Americans to strike down other **barriers** in the struggle for equality. People realized they could accomplish a great deal if they acted together and did not act violently.

Further reading:

Glenda A. Rabby, "Out of the Past: The Civil Rights Movement in Tallahassee, Florida," Ph.D. dissertation, The Florida State University, 1984; Gregory B. Padgett, "C. K. Steele and the Tallahassee Bus Boycott," M.A. Thesis, The Florida State University, 1977.

45.

ST. AUGUSTINE, FLORIDA, AND THE CIVIL RIGHTS MOVEMENT, 1963-1964

Dr. Martin Luther King, Jr., in St. Augustine after the demonstrations at the beach in 1964
Florida State Archives

BECAUSE OF THE COLOR OF THEIR SKIN, African Americans who lived in the South could not eat at the same restaurants or stay at the same hotels as whites. When they wanted to swim, they had to go to the "Negro beach" or "colored swimming pool." In 1964, African Americans hoped that Congress would pass a new **Civil Rights Act** that would change how whites treated them. This new law would guarantee everyone the right to use the same restaurants, motels, public beaches, and pools and to attend the same movie theaters.

Some whites in St. Augustine, Florida, however, were determined to keep things as

DISCUSSION TOPICS: As you read this chapter, think about the answers to these questions: 1. Look at the photograph of the African Americans demonstrating in front of a store. How do you think the demonstrators felt during that march? 2. Do you think it helps when well-known leaders from outside Florida, for example Dr. Martin Luther King, Jr., and Jesse Jackson, come to this state to lead demonstrations? 3. Can you think of any demonstrations by other people around the United States, for example Native Americans?

> *VOCABULARY*
> Civil Rights Act, klansmen,
> white supremacists

they were and were opposed to the Civil Rights Act of 1964. They did not want African Americans to use their beaches and theaters. They did not want to have to associate with African Americans on a social basis.

St. Augustine African Americans were determined to fight for equality. They wanted to bring an end to segregated schools and other facilities. Throughout 1963 and 1964 African Americans in St. Augustine conducted an economic boycott. They refused to buy from white businesses and encouraged Northern whites not to vacation in St. Augustine. The city was a major tourist area and a favorite vacation spot for many white northerners.

Dr. Martin Luther King, Jr., and the Southern Christian Leadership Conference (SCLC) came to St. Augustine to help African Americans fight for their civil rights. When African Americans tried to use the white part

of St. Augustine Beach on June 25, 1964, angry whites attacked them.

Later on that night, after listening to a speech from Dr. King, civil rights workers Fred Shuttlesworth, Andrew Young, and Hosea Williams led some 300 African Americans and 50 whites on a march through downtown St. Augustine. Reverend King did not march with them because it was too dangerous.

When the marchers approached the plaza, they were attacked by approximately 500 whites who had been listening to speeches from **klansmen** and **white supremacists**. A white reporter helped a young African American girl to get away from the mob after she had been injured and was crying for help; her dress was torn and her shoulder was bleeding. The white mob attacked the reporter for helping the young girl and kicked him in the stomach many times.

Picketing of Tallahassee stores because of lack of progress in desegregating the lunch counters at Neisner's, McCrory's, F.W. Woolworth's, Walgreen's and Sears' stores, Dec. 6-7, 1960

Florida State Archives

114

St. Augustine was the scene of marches and demonstrations.
Florida State Archives

The police could not protect the civil rights marchers, who were outnumbered by the angry white mob. African Americans ran to get away from the angry whites. Many marchers were injured, and 18 of them were taken to the hospital. Dr. King, who was very upset about the violence, thought that St. Augustine whites were worse than Birmingham whites. Dr. King asked President Lyndon Johnson to send federal troops to help them. Pictures from the riots appeared in newspapers all across the country. Violence against African Americans continued for a long time.

St. Augustine whites were stubborn. Things did not change immediately for African Americans in the city, but progress was made. The economic boycott hurt the community. Businessmen began to permit African Americans to eat in their restaurants and to stay in their hotels even though they did not like it. Some historians believe that the activities in St. Augustine played a role in convincing Congress to pass the Civil Rights Act of 1964. President Lyndon Johnson signed the Civil Rights Act into law on July 2, 1964.

Further reading:
David R. Colburn, *Racial Change & Community Crisis: St. Augustine, Florida, 1877-1980* (Gainesville: University of Florida Press, 1991).

46.

TWO AFRICAN AMERICAN WAR HEROES, 1968-1969

WAR CAN BE A TERRIBLE EXPERIENCE for those who go through it. Men and women don't usually know how they will react as soldiers when bombs are going off around them or enemy soldiers are shooting at them or their fellow soldiers are close to death. Two young African Americans from Florida faced their greatest challenge during the Vietnam War and passed the test.

Clifford Chester Sims was born in Port St. Joe, Florida, on June 18, 1942. After graduating from Washington High School, he joined the Army, trained at Fort Jackson in South Carolina, and went with his fellow soldiers to Vietnam in December 1967.

Two months later, on February 21, 1968, he was leading his **squad** of soldiers against a group of enemy soldiers who were firing their guns at his squad. Sims skillfully led his men to beat back the enemy and proceed in their survey of the area. As he was leading his men, he heard a sound that told him that a **booby trap** was about to go off; a booby trap is some type of bomb that is often hidden and which will explode when touched or approached.

When Sims realized that the bomb was about to explode, he quickly called out a warning to his men and threw himself onto the bomb in order to protect his fellow soldiers. By throwing himself onto the bomb and taking the full force of the explosion,

Clifford Chester Sims, winner of the Medal of Honor.
State of Florida, Dept. of Military Affairs

Sims gave up his life in order to save the men he was leading. He died that they might live. For his great courage the U.S. government awarded Clifford Chester Sims the Medal of Honor, the highest honor our nation can give

DISCUSSION TOPICS: As you read this chapter, think about the answers to these questions: 1. How do we honor soldiers who die in war? 2. Why do you think people have such strong feelings in front of the Vietnam War Memorial? 3. Why do we rename places like towns or cities?

> *VOCABULARY*
> squad, booby trap,
> machine gunner, hand grenades

116

a soldier. Sims is buried in Barrancas National Cemetery in Pensacola, Florida.

The other African American soldier from Florida who received the Medal of Honor for his actions during the Vietnam War was Robert H. Jenkins, Jr. He was born June 1, 1948, in the small town of Interlachen in Putnam County, Florida. He graduated from Palatka Central Academy, which at that time was an all-African American school. It is now an integrated school and has been renamed Robert Jenkins Middle School in his honor.

After graduation, Jenkins joined the Marines and did his training at Parris Island in South Carolina. In July 1968, he went to Vietnam with his fellow Marines. In March 1969, he was serving as a **machine gunner** against a group of enemy soldiers firing guns and throwing **hand grenades**. One enemy soldier threw a hand grenade into the place where Jenkins and another Marine were stationed. Fully aware of what he was doing, Jenkins took hold of his fellow Marine, pushed him to the ground, and threw himself on top of the man to protect him from the exploding hand grenade. The tremendous force of the explosion wounded Jenkins so severely that he died soon after.

For his bravery in saving the life of another Marine at the risk of his own life, the U.S. government awarded Robert Jenkins, Jr., the Medal of Honor. He is buried in Sister Spring Cemetery in Interlachen, Florida.

Further reading:
Florida Medal of Honor Recipients (St. Augustine, FL: State Arsenal, 198- .

Robert H. Jenkins, Jr., winner of the Medal of Honor
State of Florida, Dept. of Military Affairs

47.

DANIEL "CHAPPIE" JAMES, JR., AMERICA'S FIRST AFRICAN AMERICAN FOUR-STAR GENERAL, 1920-1978

Daniel "Chappie" James, Jr.
Florida State Archives

"DAN BABY" WATCHED AS THE AIRPLANES flew overhead and dreamed of the day when he would be in the cockpit. He could not wait. More than anything he wanted to fly. Daniel "Chappie" James, Jr., was born and raised in Pensacola, Florida, the naval aviation center of the United States. At the time there were no African American pilots in the U.S. military, but Daniel's parents had taught

him to follow his dreams.

Daniel James was the 17th child born to Lillie and Daniel James, Sr. His father worked at the gas plant, and his mother operated a school. His parents were strict. They taught him how to deal with racism and discrimination and gave him an appreciation for hard work. His mother added an 11th Commandment to the ten he had already learned in church: "Thou shall not quit." She encour-

DISCUSSION TOPICS: As you read this chapter, think about the answers to these questions: 1. Why do you think some people want to fly airplanes? 2. If you had an "Eleventh Commandment" to give to your children some day, what would it be? 3. Do you know of any mottoes that anyone lives by?

aged him to "prove to the world that you can compete on an equal basis."

When Daniel entered high school, he no longer wanted to be called by his nickname "Dan Baby." He announced to his family and friends that he was adopting his older brother Charles's nickname, "Chappie." Charles had been a star athlete in college. Dan Baby was now known as "Little Chappie." Little Chappie liked high school. He sang in the choir and played both football and basketball, but he still dreamed of flying. He even did chores for the pilots at the airbase in return for rides in their planes. After graduating from high school in 1937, Chappie James attended Tuskegee Institute in Tuskegee, Alabama. At 6'4" he had grown tall and strong. He played football and basketball at Tuskegee, but also had to work to help pay the cost of his education. He still dreamed of flying someday, but knew it would be difficult. Racism and discrimination stood in his way. There was no United States Air Force yet, and African Americans were not allowed in the **Army Air Corps**. Some white people believed that African Americans could not learn to fly planes.

While Chappie was at Tuskegee Institute, his dream of becoming a pilot became stronger when, in 1939, a Civilian Pilot Training Program was established there. Chappie James enrolled and caught on very quickly; flying planes was easy for him. His teachers were impressed, but Chappie and the other African Americans in the training program wanted to impress America. They wanted to join the Army Air Corps to convince white America that African Americans could indeed fly planes.

Finally in 1941 African Americans were accepted in the Army Air Corps with the formation of the 99th Pursuit Squadron. Chappie graduated from the Civilian Pilot Training Program in January 1943 and entered the air cadet program for African Americans. He successfully completed training and became an officer in the Army Air Corps in July 1943.

Even though Chappie James was willing to die for his country, which was now involved in World War II, he was not treated as an equal. But his parents had taught him that he was an American and that he was to love and serve his country. And serve his country he would. As a **fighter pilot**, Chappie James served in the Korean War and the Vietnam War. In 1950, he was seriously injured when his two-seater T-33 failed to operate properly. Because of his size and his strength he managed to pull himself and his unconscious co-pilot out of the plane before it exploded. In addition to crushing a **vertebra** in his back, Chappie was severely burned. He received the Distinguished Service Medal for bravery for his heroic efforts.

He received many other medals and honors. During the Vietnam War, Chappie was appointed Commander of the North American Air Defense Command. In 1975, Chappie James became the first African American four-star general in United States history.

Further reading:
James R. McGovern, *Black Eagle: General Daniel "Chappie" James, Jr.* (Tuscaloosa: University of Alabama Press, 1985); J. Alfred Phelps, *Chappie: The Life and Times of Daniel James, Jr.* (Novato, CA: Presidio Press, 1991).

48.
GWENDOLYN SAWYER CHERRY, EDUCATOR, ATTORNEY, POLITICIAN, 1923-1979

Gwendolyn Sawyer Cherry
Florida State Archives

GWENDOLYN SAWYER CHERRY WAS BORN in Miami, Florida, August 27, 1923. Her mother, Alberta Sawyer, owned and operated a hotel, and her father, William B., was the first African American doctor in Dade County. Gwendolyn and her three brothers and sisters had many advantages as they were growing up. Their parents tried to give them the best and to protect them as much as possible from racism.

Gwendolyn began school in Miami, but later her parents sent her to school in Jamaica, New York. They believed that she could get a better education there. After graduating from high school, she enrolled at

DISCUSSION TOPICS: As you read this chapter, think about the answers to these questions: 1. Who are the role models in your life? 2. What does a trail blazer do? 3. What difference can an African American make by serving in the state legislature?

VOCABULARY
role model, civil rights, trail blazer

Florida Agricultural and Mechanical University (FAMU) in Tallahassee, Florida, where she studied chemistry and biology and graduated in 1946. Four years later, she earned a Master's degree in Human Relations from New York University.

For 18 years Ms. Cherry taught science to African American students in Miami, encouraging them to set high goals and then to do their best to achieve those goals. She encouraged them to become lawyers and doctors. Ms. Cherry, an excellent **role model** for her students, decided to follow her own advice and applied for law school. She became the first African American to attend the University of Miami Law School. After one year there, she transferred to FAMU Law School, where she excelled. She graduated at the top of her class in 1965 and passed the Florida bar exam on her first try.

Gwendolyn Cherry worked in **civil rights**, taught students at FAMU's Law School, and was a practicing attorney before she decided to run for the state legislature in 1970. After defeating her opponent and winning the right to represent Florida's 96th district, Gwendolyn Cherry became the first African American woman elected to the Florida state legislature. As a legislator she supported such issues as women's and minority rights, prison reform, and the rights of children.

Gwendolyn Sawyer Cherry is considered a **trail blazer** because she accomplished so much in spite of the color of her skin and her gender. She created opportunities and inspired others to do the same. Her life of service was cut short, however, in 1979, when she was killed in an automobile accident in Tallahassee, Florida, at the age of 56. In 1991, the new Department of Education Child Development Center in Tallahassee was named in her honor because in 1971 she had introduced the first laws for state-provided child care in Florida.

Further reading:
Roderick D. Waters, "Gwendolyn Cherry: Educator, Attorney and the First African American Female Legislator in The History of Florida," M.A. Thesis, The Florida State University, 1990.

49.
MARY LITTLEJOHN SINGLETON, CITY COUNCILWOMAN, STATE LEGISLATOR, 1926-1980

MARY LITTLEJOHN SINGLETON WAS BORN in Jacksonville, Florida, in 1926. Her family was quite well off financially as her father owned a prosperous barbershop that served whites. Mary attended Boylan Haven Industrial Training School, a private school in Jacksonville. After graduating from Boylan Haven, she attended Booker T. Washington's alma mater, Hampton Institute in Hampton, Virginia. Mary studied **horticulture**, which is the science of growing plants, fruits, and vegetables. At the end of her second year at Hampton, she transferred to Florida Agricultural and Mechanical University and earned a Bachelor of Arts (B.A.) degree in 1949. She then became a school teacher.

Mary later married Isadore Singleton, the owner of five barbecue restaurants. In 1967, three years after her husband died, Ms. Singleton decided to run for the Jacksonville **City Council** and won. Her victory made her one of the first African Americans, along with Sallye Mathis, to sit on the City Council in more than 60 years.

Mary Littlejohn Singleton
Florida State Archives

DISCUSSION TOPICS: As you read this chapter, think about the answers to these questions: 1. What does it mean to say that a person is "color blind" when it comes to people? 2. Mary Singleton's father owned a prosperous barbershop. If he had been a barber 100 years ago, he might have had an outdoor barbershop, as pictured in the photograph. Describe such an outdoor barbershop from the photograph. 3. Would you ever be interested in running for election in some position, either in school or much later in your career?

> *VOCABULARY*
> horticulture, City Council, congress-woman, state supervisor of elections, lieutenant governor, color blind

Outdoor barber shop
Florida State Archives

A seat on the Jacksonville City Council was the beginning of a political career for Ms. Singleton. In 1972, she was elected to the Florida House of Representatives. As a **congresswoman**, Ms. Singleton was a strong supporter of education and served as vice chairman of the House Committee on Education.

In 1976, Florida Secretary of State Bruce Smathers appointed Ms. Singleton to the post of Florida **state supervisor of elections**. Her goal was to revise the state's electoral codes and to computerize the state's 67 elections offices. She achieved another first in 1978 when former governor Claude Kirk asked her to run as his **lieutenant governor** in his unsuccessful bid to become Florida's governor once again. In 1979, Florida State Comptroller Gerald Lewis named Ms. Singleton to direct the state's Banking and Finance Division. She held this position until 1980, when she died of cancer at the age of 54.

Ms. Singleton is remembered as a trail blazer and as someone who could bring opposing sides, for example African Americans and whites, together. She believed in the rights of all people regardless of the color of their skin. Four former Jacksonville mayors said that Ms. Singleton was **color blind** and that "she had a clear vision of what community relations and harmony in Jacksonville could and should be." She worked hard to improve race relations in her hometown. Jacksonville Mayor Jake Godbold nominated her to the Florida Women's Hall of Fame in 1982.

In 1991, the first Mary L. Singleton Memorial for Justice, Peace and Social Harmony was held in Jacksonville. Since then, many African Americans and whites have come together to honor and to share their memories of Mary Littlejohn Singleton, a great woman.

Further reading:

Barbara H. Walch, "Sallye B. Mathis and Mary L. Singleton: Black Pioneers on the Jacksonville, Florida City Council," M.A. Thesis, The University of Florida, 1988; *Florida Times-Union*, February 1, 1991; January 31, 1992; February 9, 1992.

50.
JOSEPH W. HATCHETT, FLORIDA'S FIRST AFRICAN AMERICAN SUPREME COURT JUSTICE, 1932-

Judge Joseph W. Hatchett
Florida State Archives

JOSEPH W. HATCHETT MADE HISTORY when he was appointed to the Florida Supreme Court in 1975. Not only was he the first African American to serve as a **justice** in Florida, but he was also the first African American to sit on the Supreme Court in any Southern state.

Joseph Hatchett was born in Clearwater, Florida, in 1932. His mother worked as a maid, and his father picked fruit. Even though they were poor, his parents taught Joseph and his three brothers and sisters always to do their best. If they worked hard and studied, they would get ahead. While only a young boy, Joseph learned to believe in the American Dream that through hard work

DISCUSSION TOPICS: As you read this chapter, think about the answers to these questions: 1. How was Joseph W. Hatchett able to go so far even though his mother was a maid and his father picked fruit? 2. What do you think the American Dream is? 3. The word *magistrate* comes from a Latin word that means "teacher"; how is a magistrate like a teacher?

anyone can become successful. Joseph attended school in his hometown and dreamed of attending college. His dream came true when he enrolled at Florida Agricultural and Mechanical University (FAMU) in 1950. At FAMU he participated in the Reserve Officers' Training Corps (ROTC). After graduating from FAMU in 1954, he received a **commission** in the United States Army. Joseph thought about making the military his career, but after spending two very cold winters in Germany he changed his mind.

In 1956, Joseph left the military and entered Howard University Law School in Washington, D.C. He studied civil rights law and graduated in 1959. After law school he set up an office in Daytona Beach, Florida, where he practiced for seven years. In 1966, he was appointed an Assistant United States Attorney in Jacksonville. From 1971 until 1975, he served as a U.S. **Magistrate** for the Middle District of Florida.

The Governor of Florida, Reubin Askew, appointed Joseph Hatchett to the Florida Supreme Court in 1975. To keep his position as a Supreme Court justice, however, Judge Hatchett had to seek reelection. He was successful in his reelection campaign and became the first African American since Reconstruction to be elected to a statewide office. This is what he said about his victory: "If it has any value, it is the value some young person could get in terms of motivation, knowing they can succeed in spite of being poor and black." Judge Hatchett served on the Supreme Court until 1979.

Even President Jimmy Carter was impressed with Judge Hatchett. In 1979, President Carter chose him to serve as a **federal circuit judge** on the Fifth United States Circuit Court of Appeals. Judge Hatchett, who currently serves on the Eleventh U.S. Circuit Court of Appeals, has been an inspiration to thousands of African Americans. He is an example of what one can achieve in spite of poverty and racial discrimination.

Further reading:
Tallahassee Democrat, September 2 & 8, 1975; October 24, 1975.

51.

LEANDER SHAW, CHIEF JUSTICE OF THE FLORIDA SUPREME COURT,1930-

Chief Justice Leander Shaw, Jr.
Florida State Archives

IN JULY 1990, SUPREME COURT JUSTICE LEANDER SHAW became the first African American to serve as **Chief Justice** of the Florida Supreme Court.

DISCUSSION TOPICS: As you read this chapter, think about the answers to these questions: 1. Do you think that Leander Shaw should have walked out of the hotel when he was told he had to take the Florida bar exam in a different room? 2. A lawyer like Leander Shaw might have to argue that African American workers deserve better housing than the shacks pictured on page 127. What arguments might he use? 3. If you were a judge, what do you think your hardest cases would be?

Born in Salem, Virginia, Leander Shaw was raised in Lexington, Virginia, where his father was a high school principal. When Leander was a young boy, he shined shoes to earn money, but also found time to watch football games at the Virginia Military Institute.

Leander attended West Virginia State

126

Shacks where African American farm workers lived
Courtesy, Tampa-Hillsborough County Public Library System

College, where he participated in the Reserve Officers Training Corps (ROTC). He often wondered if he was getting as good an education as white students, but at an ROTC camp in Oklahoma he competed very well with white students. After graduating from college, Leander served as an officer in the Army for two years.

Shaw completed his law degree at Howard University in Washington, D.C., and moved to Tallahassee, Florida. For three years he taught at the Florida Agricultural and Mechanical University School of Law, and then in 1960 decided to take the Florida bar exam, which was being given in a Miami hotel. He and other African Americans there experienced discrimination when they were told that they had to take the exam in a different room from the whites. Several of the African Americans left rather than give in to discrimination. It was a tough decision for Shaw, but he had faced discrimination all his life and decided to stay and take the exam. He passed.

Shaw then became a lawyer in Jacksonville, where he still faced **prejudice**. For instance, a white court clerk refused to accept legal papers that Shaw was trying to file. Shaw often represented African Americans who were fighting for their civil rights. In 1965, he became an assistant **public defender**.

Florida Governor Bob Graham appointed Leander Shaw to the 1st District Court of Appeals in 1979. Four years later, in 1983, Judge Shaw became only the second African American to sit on the Florida Supreme Court. Floridians voted to keep him as a justice in 1984 and again in 1990. The other Supreme Court Justices voted him to be their Chief Justice in 1990.

Judge Leander Shaw did not allow racism and discrimination to keep him from following his dreams. He performed his job with dignity and brought a different point of view to the Supreme Court. He serves as an excellent role model to African American youth all across the state.

Further reading:
Florida Times-Union, September 3, 1990; July 14, 1990.

52.

CARRIE PITTMAN MEEK,
UNITED STATES CONGRESSWOMAN, 1926-

Carrie P. Meek
Florida State Archives

IN 1992, STATE SENATOR CARRIE MEEK won the right to represent Florida in the United States Congress, along with Corrine Brown and Alcee Hastings. In doing so they became the first African Americans since Josiah T. Walls (who served in the 1870s) to represent Florida in Washington, D.C.

Carrie Pittman Meek was born in Tallahassee, Florida, in 1926. She lived with her parents and 11 brothers and sisters not far from the capitol building in a **ghetto** area called Black Bottom. Her father was a farmer, and her mother washed clothes for others. Carrie was nicknamed "Tot" and was considered a tomboy. She wanted to become a **veterinarian** when she grew up.

DISCUSSION TOPICS: As you read this chapter, think about the answers to these questions: 1. Do you know anyone who has ever won a varsity letter in any sport? 2. What do you think someone like Carrie Meek learned from playing basketball and softball? 3. Carrie Meek introduced some bills to help women. How could she help such women pictured in the photograph on page 129?

VOCABULARY
ghetto, veterinarian, varsity letter,
politician, state legislator,
affordable housing

Workers sorting flowers
Courtesy, Tampa-Hillsborough County Public Library System

She attended Florida Agricultural and Mechanical University (FAMU) and majored in physical education. She was a good student, but also found time for sports. Carrie was an excellent athlete and participated in varsity basketball, softball, and track. She earned a **varsity letter** in track and field and was elected to FAMU's Sports Hall of Fame. In 1948, she earned a Master's degree from the University of Michigan.

Ms. Meek worked at Bethune-Cookman College in Daytona Beach and became friends with Mary McLeod Bethune. Ms. Bethune became her heroine and role model. In 1961, Ms. Meek got a job at Miami-Dade Community College in Miami, Florida, and through hard work was promoted to assistant to the president.

When state congresswoman Gwendolyn Cherry was killed in an automobile accident in 1979, Ms. Meek decided that she could best represent her district, even though she was not well known and did not have the support of many of Miami's influential African Americans. But she believed in herself and defeated 13 other candidates. In 1982, she became the first African American woman elected to the Florida Senate.

Ms. Meek has been a very effective **politician**. During her term as a **state legislator**, she introduced bills to aid women and minority business owners, to provide **affordable housing**, and to improve education. She made history when she won the 1992 U.S. Congressional race. When Ms. Meek won 83% of the vote and defeated three other candidates, she and Corrine Brown of Jacksonville became the first African American congresswomen from Florida.

Further reading:
"First Black Woman in Florida's History Elected to Become Member of Congress," *Jet* 82 (September 28, 1992), pp. 34-37; *Time*, November 2, 1992; Allen Morris, *A Changing Pattern: Women in the Legislature* (Tallahassee: 1991).

53.

JESSE J. McCRARY, JR., FLORIDA'S FIRST AFRICAN AMERICAN CABINET MEMBER SINCE RECONSTRUCTION, 1937-

Florida Secretary of State Jesse J. McCrary, Jr.
Florida State Archives

IN 1978, GOVERNOR REUBIN ASKEW appointed Miami attorney Jesse J. McCrary, Jr., Secretary of the State of Florida. Attorney McCrary became only the second African American to serve as a member of the Florida cabinet. Jonathan Gibbs, who served during Reconstruction, was Florida's first African American to hold a cabinet position.

Jesse McCrary was born in Blichton, Florida, in Marion County. His father was a Baptist minister and hoped that his son would follow in his footsteps. Jesse, however, planned on becoming a doctor. Those plans changed when he realized that he could not stand the sight of blood.

After graduating from high school, Jesse enrolled at Florida Agricultural and Mechanical University (FAMU) in Tallahassee. He

DISCUSSION TOPICS: As you read this chapter, think about the answers to these questions: 1. What do you think Jesse McCrary meant when he thought of himself as "the link between the 'establishment and the ghetto'"? 2. What does the term "public servant" mean? 3. Describe the graph here in terms of what peoples earn what money.

VOCABULARY
political science, honor court, advocate

130

graduated in 1960 with a **political science** degree. According to McCrary, he developed "a feel for law and order" while serving on the **honor court** at FAMU. This may have played a role in his decision to become a lawyer. He entered FAMU's law school and graduated in 1965.

His ability was recognized almost immediately. State Attorney General Earl Faircloth appointed him assistant attorney general and assigned him to Miami. He held this position for several years. He made

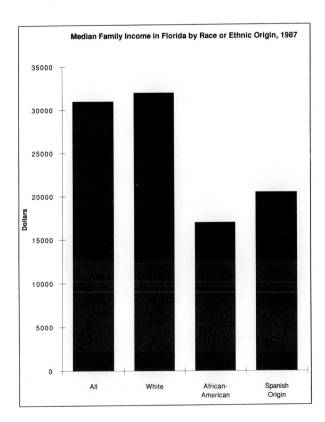

history when as an assistant attorney general he became the first African American to represent Florida before the United States Supreme Court.

Jesse McCrary wanted very much to bring African Americans and whites together to work out their differences. In 1971, he was appointed to head a commission to study the causes of riots in Opa-Locka's black community. He often served as an **advocate** on behalf of poor African Americans and considered himself as "the link between the 'establishment and the ghetto.' "

Jesse McCrary was an active public servant. He was a member of several important committees including the Commission on Judicial Reform, the Capital Punishment Study Commision and the Constitution Revision Commission. He was a partner in the law firm of McCrary, Berkowitz and Davis when Governor Askew appointed him Secretary of State in 1978. The appointment, however, was a temporary one. Serving only until January 1979, McCrary was to complete the term of Bruce Smathers, who had resigned to run for the governorship of Florida. McCrary was sworn in by the only African American on Florida's Supreme Court, Justice Joseph Hatchett. McCrary's father, Jessie McCrary, Sr., gave the prayer at the swearing-in ceremony.

Further reading:
Tallahassee Democrat July 20, 1978; *Florida Flambeau* July 20, 1978; *The Miami Herald* July 20, 1978.

54.
HARRY KTHAW SINGLETARY, JR., SECRETARY OF THE FLORIDA DEPARTMENT OF CORRECTIONS, 1946-

Harry K. Singletary, Jr.

FLORIDA GOVERNOR LAWTON CHILES named Harry Kthaw Singletary, Jr., Secretary for the Florida **Department of Corrections** in 1991. Mr. Singletary became the first African American to head the Florida Department of Corrections.

Harry Singletary grew up in Tarpon Springs, Florida, with his three sisters. His father had to quit his job when he became very ill. His mother supported the family financially with the money she earned as a housekeeper and a baby sitter. Harry admired his father for his love of books and his mother for her mental toughness. They were his role models. Harry's parents passed their

DISCUSSION TOPICS: As you read this chapter, think about the answers to these questions: 1. Have you ever known anyone who went to college on a scholarship? What kind of scholarship was it? 2. Harry Kthaw Singletary, Jr., has an unusual second name. Do you know anyone with an unusual name? What does that person's name mean? 3. What are some ways to handle a slur when you hear one?

> *VOCABULARY*
> Department of Corrections, slur,
> probation, budget

Florida State Prison at Raiford
Florida State Archives

love and thirst for knowledge and learning to their four children. Even though they were poor, there was more than enough love to go around in the Singletary household. Harry and his sisters received guidance, encouragement, and support from their parents.

Harry grew up in a segregated society. However, his parents prepared him and his sisters for the challenges they would face based on the climate of racial separation and discrimination. The parents taught their children that they were everyone's equal regardless of race, creed, color or station in life. His parents nurtured their self-esteem.

His parents also would not allow anyone to use the word "can't" in the Singletary household. It was the parents' belief that once this word was used, an individual was automatically defeated. The important words were "try" and "persevere."

From his parents he learned that education was the key to a better life and was encouraged to study and make good grades. Even though he knew that his parents could not afford to send him, he wanted to go to college.

Harry won a basketball scholarship to Kentucky State College, but transferred after two years to Florida Presbyterian College (now Eckerd College) in St. Petersburg. He became the first African American to play basketball at a predominantly white college in Florida. But racism reared its ugly head on the basketball court.

During a championship game, Harry's team was behind in points when he was fouled. Harry was standing at the free-throw line when a white player made a racial **slur**. Harry did not lose his cool. He made both free throws and played even harder than before. When the game ended, Harry had scored 35 points. His team won the game as well as the championship title. He loved basketball, but education was important too. Harry graduated from Florida Presbyterian College in 1968 and received his Master's degree from the University of Chicago in 1971.

Mr. Singletary, as a juvenile corrections officer, spent most of his career working with young people who had broken the law, first in Illinois and then in Florida. From 1979 to 1983 Mr. Singletary served as the Regional Director of Region Five for the Florida Department of Corrections. In September 1983, he was appointed Assistant Secretary for

Operations with the department. When Governor Chiles appointed Mr. Singletary Secretary for the Department of Corrections in April 1991, he became the highest-ranking African American in Florida's corrections system.

As Secretary of the Florida Department of Corrections, Mr. Singletary is in charge of more than 20,000 staff members, 49,000 inmates, and 100,000 men, women, and children on **probation**. He is also in charge of a billion-dollar **budget**. He has a lot of responsibility.

When Mr. Singletary was working directly with young people who had committed crimes, he tried to help them to change the direction of their lives. He wanted them to have "a fighting chance." Because he still believed that education was the key, he tried to make sure that education was available for those juveniles in prison. He said: "If there is any place to turn the kids around, this is the place. We don't want the criminals to come in here illiterate and go out illiterate." But Mr. Singletary wanted them to learn responsibility as well as how to learn to read and write.

Harry Singletary has worked hard to get to where he is today. He has experienced bad luck and hard times as well as racism. But he did not let these potential obstacles get in his way. He did not give up. Today as Secretary for the Florida Department of Corrections, Mr. Singletary serves as a role model to thousands of African Americans across the state. In 1992, Mr. Singletary was honored nationally when the American Correctional Association awarded him the E. R. Cass Correctional Award, the highest and most prestigious award in the field of corrections.

Further reading:
Bob Chick, "Harry Singletary," *The Floridian* December 28, 1980, pp. 22-25.

CALENDAR

JANUARY

Jan. 1, 1863 - President Lincoln signed the Emancipation Proclamation freeing the slaves in the Confederate states, including Florida.

Jan. 3, 1861 - A meeting of delegates from around Florida debated whether to leave the union after Abraham Lincoln was elected president of the United States.

Jan. 4, 1940 - Florida African American attorney S. D. McGill made an appeal before the United States Supreme Court concerning the so-called "Pompano Boys." See Feb. 12, 1940, below and p. 102.

Jan. 6, 1926 - The students at what would become Florida A&M University saw their first motion picture on campus, *The Ten Commandments*.

Jan. 7 - Zora Neale Hurston was born in Eatonville, Florida, in 1891 or 1901.

Jan. 8, 1957 - In his inaugural speech, Governor LeRoy Collins said that integration was coming to Florida and that the state should prepare for it.

Jan. 10 - (1) In **1861**, Florida voted to leave (secede from) the United States after Abraham Lincoln was elected president. (2) In **1983**, Governor Bob Graham appointed to the Florida Supreme Court Leander J. Shaw, Jr., a man who would become the state's first African American Chief Justice in 1990.

Jan. 11, 1958 - Althea Gibson of Florida A&M University was named the Female Athlete of the Year by the Associated Press; she was the first African American to win the important singles tennis tournament at Wimbledon, England.

Jan. 16, 1866 - The Florida Legislature passed the first law for the education of African Americans in the state, authorizing a superintendent to organize schools for African Americans.

Jan. 20, 1868 - The state constitutional convention, at which Josiah Walls represented many African Americans in Alachua County and which had 18 African Americans, met in Tallahassee.

Jan. 21, 1955 - Turner Radford, a railroad switchman in Jacksonville, saved two young children and a blind man from a burning house, for which act the Carnegie Hero Fund Commission honored Radford.

Jan. 23 - (1) In **1873**, Jonathan Gibbs began serving as Florida's Superintendent of Public Instruction. See p.44. (2) In **1890**, Blanche Armwood, an important educator and leader, was born in Tampa, Florida, See p. 87.

Jan. 25, 1959 - Mark Duper, skilled wide receiver of the Miami Dolphins professional football team, was born in Pineville, Louisiana.

Jan. 26, 1864 - J.R.E. Lee, who would become the third president of what would become Florida A&M University, was born a slave on a ranch in Texas.

Jan. 28 - (1) In **1934**, Bill White, who would become the first black president of baseball's National League, was born in Lakewood, Florida. (2) In **1960**, the distinguished African American writer Zora Neale Hurston died in Fort Pierce, Florida.

Jan. 31, 1865 - Congress passed the Thirteenth Amendment. When it was later ratified by the states, it abolished slavery in the United States.

FEBRUARY
BLACK HISTORY MONTH

Fishing on the St. Johns River
Florida State Archives

Feb. 2 - (1) In **1894**, officials opened St. Peter Claver School in Tampa, the oldest African American school, public or private, still operating in Hillsborough County. See p. 175 [#135] (2) In **1968**, Robert H. Jenkins, Jr., of Interlachen, Florida, joined the U.S. Naval Service in Jacksonville. He went on to serve in the Vietnam War, where he died in 1969 after saving the life of a fellow Marine, for which he received the Medal of Honor. See p. 117

Feb. 3, 1989 - Bill White, was who born in Lakewood, Florida, became the first black president of baseball's National League.

Feb. 4 - (1) In 1861, representatives from Florida met in Alabama with other southerners to draw up a constitution for the Confederate States of America. (2) In **1983**, a Miami jury acquitted Federal Judge Alcee Hastings of criminal charges.

Feb. 7, 1951 - The Florida A&M College Hospital was formally dedicated in Tallahassee.

Feb. 8, 1954 - Finley Kicklighter, an African American laborer, saved a seven-year-old boy from being killed by a train in St. Petersburg, Florida, when the boy tensed up with fright. The Carnegie Hero Fund Commission honored Kicklighter for his courage.

Feb. 11, 1920 - Daniel "Chappie" James, Jr., the first African American four-star general in U.S. military history, was born in Pensacola, Florida.

Feb. 12 -(1) In **1894**, St. Peter Claver School in Tampa was burned by arsonists but it was rebuilt and reopened. See p. 175. [#135] (2) In **1940**, the U.S. Supreme Court reversed the decision of the Florida Supreme Court in a case involving four young African American men. See p. 102.

Feb. 13, 1960 - The first lunch-counter sit-in in Tallahassee began.

Feb. 14, 1930 - Famous musician Dwike Mitchell was born in Dunedin, Florida. For more about him see William Zinsser, *Willie and Dwike* (New York: Harper & Row, 1984).

Feb. 20 - (1) In **1864**, Union troops, including many African Americans, fought Confederate troops at the Battle of Olustee in north Florida. See p. 33. (2) In **1924**, actor Sidney Poitier was born in Miami.

Feb. 21, 1968 - Clifford Chester Sims, who was born and raised in Port St. Joe, Florida, died in the Vietnam War while saving the lives of the soldiers in his squad, for which he received the Medal of Honor. See p. 116.

Feb. 22, 1979 - Wilford William Lyons, an African American laborer in Cocoa, Florida, died trying to save a man who had fallen into a manhole full of dangerous fumes. The Carnegie Hero Fund Commission honored Lyons for his bravery.

Feb. 23, 1990 - The National Register of Historic Places recognized the Daytona Beach home of Dr. Howard Thurman as a National Historic Preservation Site. See #26 of the Black Trail, p. 155.

Feb. 25, 1978 - Pensacola's Daniel "Chappie" James, Jr., the first African American four-star general in U.S. military history, died of a heart attack at age 58. He was buried at Arlington National Cemetery in Virginia.

Feb. 27, 1902 - Robert Meacham, an important African American leader in Florida's Reconstruction, died in Tampa. See pp. 37–38.

Feb. 29 - (1) In 1900, sculptor Augusta Savage was born in Green Cove Springs, Florida. See p. 66. (2) In 1960, 57 young African Americans staged a "sit-in" in Tampa that led to the integration of the city's lunch counters, movie theaters, and beaches.

MARCH

Gathering sap from turpentine pines
Florida State Archives

March 1, 1949 - Mary McLeod Bethune, the founder of Bethune Cookman College in Daytona Beach, became the first African American to receive an honorary degree from a white college in the South when Rollins College in Winter Park, Florida, awarded her an honorary degree, Doctor of Humanities.

March 3, 1845 - Florida entered the Union as a slave state.

March 4, 1871 - Josiah T. Walls, Florida's first black Congressman, began serving his first term.

March 5 - (1) In 1883, the Florida legislature passed a bill that authorized money for teacher's institutes, one white and one African American. (2) In 1969, Robert H. Jenkins, Jr., of Interlachen, Florida, died in the Vietnam War after saving the life of a fellow soldier; for his bravery Jenkins received the Medal of Honor. See p. 117.

March 6, 1950 - Dr. George William Gore, Jr., was nominated to become president of Florida A&M College for Negroes.

March 10, 1863 - Two African American infantry regiments in the Civil War, First and Second South Carolina Volunteers, captured and occupied Jacksonville, Florida. That caused much panic in the state.

March 12, 1960 - Twenty-nine students were arrested for a "sit-in" at local stores in Tallahassee as they attempted to end segregation.

March 15, 1958 - Officials at Florida A&M University dedicated the Student Union Building, the Agricultural-Home Economics Building, and an addition to the dining hall.

March 17, 1946 - Baseball great Jackie Robinson played in the first racially integrated spring training game, which took place in Daytona between the Montreal Royals and the Brooklyn Dodgers. See p. 155.

March 19, 1964 - John "Pop" Lloyd, baseball great from Palatka, Florida, died in Atlantic City, NJ.

March 27, 1979 - Carrie Meek was elected to the Florida House in a special election to succeed Gwendolyn Sawyer Cherry, the first African American woman ever to serve in the Florida legislature.

March 28, 1927 - Booker T. Washington High School was opened in Miami as the first school in South Florida to provide a 12th-grade education for African American children.

March 29, 1967 - Florida is ordered to desegregate all school grades.

APRIL

An example of housing after Emancipation near Tallahassee.
Florida State Archives

April 1, 1911 - Lincoln B. Childs, M.D., a doctor who delivered hundreds of Jacksonville's African Americans, was born in Gainesville.

April 4, 1961 - Ivery W. Elps, Jr., a 38-year-old African American worker in Jacksonville, Florida, saved two men from suffocation in a huge tank full of dangerous fumes, for which the Carnegie Hero Fund Commission honored Elps.

April 6, 1944 - J.R.E. Lee, Sr., the third president of what would become Florida A&M University, died after 20 years in office

April 8, 1873 - Joseph E. Lee became a lawyer, one of the first African Americans to do so in Florida.

April 9, 1991 - The Museum of African American Art opened in Tampa on what may have been the site of the city's first public library for African Americans.

April 10, 1869 - The original Stanton High School was dedicated in Jacksonville, and, although it later burned down, a school on this site would serve African Americans until it closed in 1971. See p. 161. Stanton continues to exist.

April 11, 1903 - Alonzo S. "Jake" Gaither was born on this day. He went on to become the highly successful football coach at Florida A&M University and was elected to the National Football Foundation Hall of Fame in 1975. See pp. 97-98.

Alonzo "Jake" Gaither
Florida State Archives

April 12, 1991 - Harry K. Singletary, Jr., was named secretary for the Florida Department of Corrections by Gov. Lawton Chiles, becoming the first African American to lead the state's inmate system.

April 14, 1952 - Tony Baker, an African American worker in Marianna, Florida, saved another worker from electric shock when a derrick came into contact with a high-tension wire, for which bravery the Carnegie Hero Fund Commission honored Baker.

April 15, 1889 - A. Philip Randolph, civil rights leader, was born in Crescent City.

April 16, 1528 - Estevanico, the first known African in Florida, arrived in the Tampa Bay area with a Spanish force led by Panfilo de Narváez.

April 18, 1818 - Andrew Jackson and his troops defeated a force of Native Americans and African Americans at the Battle of Suwanee; that defeat ended the First Seminole War.

April 23, 1932 - The school that would become Florida A&M University established its first social fraternities.

April 25, 1884 - John Henry "Pop" Lloyd, the great baseball player, was born in Palatka, Florida; see p. 59

April 26, 1957 - *Time* magazine featured on its cover Florida A&M University graduate Althea Gibson after she became the first African American to win the United States Women's Open Tennis Tournament and then the Wimbledon Tennis Tournament in England.

April 30 - (1) In **1867**, Elijah Williams of Marianna, Florida, was granted a patent on a boat propeller. (2) In **1926**, Bessie Coleman died after her airplane crashed in Jacksonville; she may have been the first African American woman pilot in the world and flew 350 solo flights.

MAY

Tomato pickers, Dade County?
Florida State Archives

May 1, 1528 - Estevanico, the first known African in Florida, began a long overland trip from Tampa to Mexico with a Spanish force led by Panfilo de Narváez.

May 9, 1862 - Florida slaves were almost freed on this day when Major General David Hunter of the Union Army proclaimed that the slaves in Florida, Georgia, and South Carolina were free; President Lincoln overruled Hunter and postponed the slaves' freedom.

May 12, 1906 - James Weldon Johnson left New York City to become a U.S. consul in Venezuela.

May 14, 1952 - President Gore of Florida A&M College in Tallahassee held the school's first Community Day in which citizens of the city and state visited the school to observe its progress and needs.

May 17 - (1) A. Philip Randolph, labor leader and civil rights pioneer who was born in Florida, died in **1979**. (2) On May 17, **1954**, the U.S. Supreme Court ruled that racial segregation in public schools was unconstitutional.

May 18, 1955 - Mary McLeod Bethune, founder and president of Bethune-Cookman College in Daytona Beach, died in Daytona Beach.

May 20 - (1) In **1865**, Union General Edward McCook in Tallahassee announced President Lincoln's Emancipation Proclamation that freed the slaves. See #127 of the Florida Black Heritage Trail. (2) In **1868**, when African Americans first served as presidential electors, Robert Meacham was a presidential elector in Florida.

May 21, 1973 - Daniel "Chappie" James, Jr., of Pensacola is promoted to lieutenant general and becomes the highest-ranking African American in the U.S. military. He would later become the first African American four-star general and the commander of the North American Air Defense Command.

May 22, 1909 - The Florida Legislature changed the name of the Colored Normal School in Tallahassee to Florida Agricultural and Mechanical College for Negroes.

May 27, 1956 - The Tallahassee bus boycott began.

Oldest member of the adult education class,
Washington School, June 17, 1935
Florida State Archives

JUNE

June 1, 1948 - Robert H. Jenkins, Jr., was born in Interlachen, Florida. He graduated from Palatka Central Academy, at the time an all-African American school, now integrated and named Robert Jenkins Middle School. While serving in the Vietnam War in 1969, he died after saving the life of a fellow soldier, for which Jenkins received the Medal of Honor. See p. 117.

June 2, 1928 - T. Thomas Fortune, distinguished journalist, died. See p 49.

June 8, 1944 - The school that would become Florida A&M University chose its fifth president, Dr. William H. Gray.

June 9 - (1) In **1892**, the State Normal and Industrial College in Tallahassee, which would later become Florida A&M University, held its first graduation. (2) In **1964**, Dr. Martin Luther King, Jr., told 300 supporters in St. Augustine that he would participate in a sit-in at a motel restaurant the next day, an announcement that led to his arrest.

June 10, 1865 - The Midway African Methodist Episcopal Church, which was organized in Duval County right after the Civil War, was the first African American independent church organized in Florida.

June 11-13, 1967 - A race riot took place in Tampa, Florida.

June 17, 1871 - James Weldon Johnson, author of the African American national anthem, "Lift Ev'ry Voice and Sing," was born in Jacksonville. See p. 75.

June 18 - (1) In **1942**, Clifford Chester Sims, who was born on this day in Port St. Joe, Florida, later died in the Vietnam War while saving the lives of the soldiers in his squad, for which he received the Medal of Honor. See p. 116. (2) In **1958**, Federal District Judge Dozier DeVane ordered the University of Florida to desegregate its graduate and professional schools.

June 19 - (1) Some Florida communities observe Emancipation Day or Juneteenth, marking the day when the slaves were freed in Texas. (2) In **1971**, ground was broken in Washington, D.C., for a statue honoring Mary McLeod Bethune, founder of Bethune-Cookman College in Daytona Beach; this was the first memorial to an African American on public land in our nation's capital.

141

June 20, 1964 - The publicity caused by civil rights protests in St. Augustine, including the arrest of Dr. Martin Luther King, Jr., did much to influence Congress to pass the Civil Rights Act on this day.

June 21, 1963 - Bob Hayes of Jacksonville, Florida, set the world record for the 100-yard dash: 9.1 seconds.

June 22, 1844 - Abolitionist Jonathan Walker sailed his boat out of Pensacola to try to free some slaves. See p. 26.

June 24, 1936 - The federal government named Mary McLeod Bethune, who founded Bethune-Cookman College in Daytona Beach, the director of Negro Affairs of the National Youth Administration. She thus became the first African American woman to receive a major appointment from the federal government. She held this position until January 1, 1944.

June 25 - (1) In **1868**, the United States Congress readmitted Florida, along with other southern states, to the Union after the Civil War on the condition that "the constitutions of said states shall never be amended or changed as to deprive any citizen or class of citizens of the United States of the right to vote in said states who are entitled to vote by the constitutions thereof herein recognized." (2) In **1961**, the Florida Ku Klux Klan joined with the United Ku Klux Klan to form the United Florida Ku Klux Klan. (3) In **1964**, when African Americans tried to use the white part of St. Augustine Beach, angry whites attacked them. See pp. 113-115.

June 26, 1938 - James Weldon Johnson died. See p. 77.

June 28 - (1) In **1980**, the 71st annual convention of the NAACP met in Miami. (2) In **1990**, Broward County got its second African American newspaper, *The Broward Times*.

JULY

Picking cotton, Leon County, Florida, circa 1900
Florida State Archives

July 1 - (1) In **1924**, J.R.E. Lee, Sr., became the third president of what would become Florida A&M University and served for 20 years. (2) In **1990**, Leander J. Shaw, Jr., became Florida's first African American Chief Justice on the state's Supreme Court.

July 3, 1836 - When Seminoles attacked Cape Florida Lighthouse at Key Biscayne, a black man on duty there was killed.

July 4, 1962 - Dr. Von D. Mizell of Fort Lauderdale led a "wade-in" to try to integrate Broward County's public beaches.

July 5, 1990 - The beating of black Haitians by white police officers outside a Cuban-owned store in North Miami helped trigger a boycott of Miami businesses by African Americans.

July 7, 1949 - H. Manning Efferson became acting president of Florida A&M College for Negroes in Tallahassee.

July 8, 1844 - Abolitionist Jonathan Walker was captured near Key West as he tried to take some slaves to freedom. See p. 26.

July 9, 1863 - Josiah Walls, who would become an important leader in Florida after the Civil War, joined the Union Army. See p. 42.

July 10 - (1) In **1875**, Mary McLeod Bethune, the founder of Bethune-Cookman College in Daytona Beach, was born in South Carolina. (2) Baseball player Dick Lundy was born in Jacksonville in **1898**, and Hal McRae was born in Avon Park in **1945**. (3) 15% of the delegates attending the Democratic National Convention that opened in Miami Beach in **1972** were African American.

July 11, 1867 - About 60 African Americans joined a similar number of white Republicans in Tallahassee for thefirst state-wide convention of the Republican Party in Florida.

July 16, 1989 - A state law renamed the University of Florida law school program in which students represent the poor "The Virgil Darnell Hawkins Civil League Clinic" in honor of the African American whom the UF law school had denied admission to in 1949, but who had gone on to become an attorney.

July 17, 1990 - African Americans in Miami began a boycott of businesses after local officials refused an official welcome to South African civil-rights crusader Nelson Mandela.

July 19, 1933 - Nathan B. Young, the second president (1901-1923) of Florida A&M College, died and was buried in Tallahassee.

July 21, 1844 - Thomas DeSaille Tucker, the first president of what would become Florida A&M University, was born in Sierra Leone, West Africa.

July 22, 1942 - Benjamin J. Baker died. He was a dedicated teacher in Punta Gorda, Florida, who was honored when the school board named Baker Academy after him. See p. 169. [#104 on Trail].

July 23, 1836 - Henry, a faithful African American man who worked at Cape Florida Lighthouse, was killed by Native Americans. See p. 21.

July 24, 1536 - Estevanico became the first black man to cross the United States and reach Mexico City.

July 27, 1816 - A shot from a gunboat in the Apalachicola River exploded the Negro Fort and killed 270 of its defenders.

July 28 - (1) In **1896**, more than one-third of the men who signed the original incorporation papers of the city of Miami were African American. (2) In **1917** James Weldon Johnson of Jacksonville helped the NAACP organize a silent march in New York City to protest violence.

AUGUST

Cutting sugar cane
Florida State Archives

Aug. 7, 1901 - Nathan B. Young was elected the second president of what would become Florida A&M University in Tallahassee.

Aug. 12, 1939 - Norman J. Masslieno, an African American fisherman in Panama City, Florida, saved another man from drowning after the man had fallen from a ship. For his bravery, the Carnegie Hero Fund Commission honored Masslieno.

Aug. 13, 1935 - Baseball great Mudcat Grant was born in Lacoochee, Florida.

Aug. 14, 1874 - Jonathan C. Gibbs died. He served as Florida's first African American cabinet official, Secretary of State from 1868 to 1873, and Superintendent of Public Instruction from January 1873 until his death. See pp. 44-45.

Aug. 17, 1953 - Theodore Henderson, Sr., saved a woman from drowning in Yeehaw, Florida, when he jumped into a canal that had snakes and alligators in order to rescue the woman from her overturned car. For that he was honored by the Carnegie Hero Fund Commission.

Aug. 20, 1565 - Black farmers and artisans help Spanish explorer Pedro Menendez in building St. Augustine, Florida.

Aug. 21, 1948 - Artis Gilmore, the highly successful basketball player at Jacksonville University and in the American Basketball Association, was born in Chipley, Florida.

Aug. 24, 1992 - Hurricane Andrew devastated much of south Dade County, destroying 42 African American churches.

Aug. 25 - (1) In **1937**, A. Philip Randolph of Crescent City, Florida, won a contract with the Pullman Company for a wage increase for porters. (2) In **1927**, Althea Gibson, who went on to Florida A&M College in Tallahassee and was named the Woman Athlete of the Year in 1957-58, was born in Silver, South Carolina.

Aug. 27 - (1) In **1923**, Gwendolyn Sawyer Cherry was born in Miami, Florida; she became the first African American to attend the University of Miami Law School and the first African American woman to be elected to the Florida state legislature. (2) In **1960**, a race riot in Jacksonville followed ten days of sit-in demonstrations.

Aug. 28, 1963 - A. Philip Randolph helped lead 250,000 Americans in a march on Washington, D.C., to demand civil and equal rights for African Americans.

Aug. 29, 1975 - General Daniel "Chappie" James, Jr., became commander-in-chief of the North American Air Defense Command and the first African American four-star general in U.S. history

Aug. 30, 1969 - Eugene Standifer, Jr., aged 15, saved two children from a burning house in Fort Myers, Florida, for which the Carnegie Hero Fund Commission honored him.

Aug. 31, 1936 - William (Big Bill) Bell became head football coach at Florida A&M College in Tallahassee. His team became conference champions in 1937 and 1938; in 1938, his team did not allow any of its opponents to score a single point.

Oyster shuckers, Apalachicola, 1909
Florida State Archives

SEPTEMBER

Sept. 1 - (1) H.E.S. Reeves established the *Miami Times*, Miami's first African American newspaper in **1923**. (2) In **1953**, Tallahassee's Florida Agricultural and Mechanical College for Negroes or Florida Agricultural and Mechanical College became Florida Agricultural and Mechanical University.

Sept. 2, 1975 - Joseph W. Hatchett became Florida's first African American Justice of the State Supreme Court.

Sept. 3, 1943 - Eddie McLaughlin, an African American rigger foreman in Jacksonville, Florida, saved a man from drowning after the man had fallen into the St. Johns River and become unconscious. The Carnegie Hero Fund Commission honored McLaughlin for his courage.

Sept. 5, 1942 - Florida's great African American writer, Zora Neale Hurston, published a story about Orlando's Lawrence Silas in *The Saturday Evening Post*.

Sept. 6, 1930 - Leander J. Shaw, Jr., a man who would become the state's first African American Chief Justice in 1990, was born in Salem, Virginia.

Sept. 13, 1843 - Zephaniah Kingsley, plantation owner on Florida's Fort George Island and an organizer of a colony in Haiti for free African Americans, died in New York City.

Sept. 15, 1990 - Dedication of the Jackie Robinson statue at Jackie Robinson Ball Park in Daytona Beach recognized the role Robinson played in integrating professional baseball in 1946. See #25 in the Black Heritage Trail.

Sept. 16, 1928 - A huge hurricane that hit Belle Glade and South Bay near Lake Okeechobee killed hundreds of African American farm workers.

Sept. 17, 1932 - Joseph W. Hatchett, who served on the Florida Supreme Court (1975-79) and as a U.S. circuit judge (1981-), was born in Clearwater, Florida. He became the first African American elected to the highest court of a state, the first elected to public office in a statewide election in the South, and the first to serve on a federal appellate court in the South.

Supreme Court Justice Joseph W. Hatchett with his family
Florida State Archives

Sept. 19, 1941 - James S. Haskins, a professor of English at the University of Florida and the author of over 100 nonfiction books, was born in Demopolis, Alabama.

Sept. 20, 1874 - Adam Paine, the first Florida African American to receive the Medal of Honor, showed great courage when his troop of soldiers was attacked by Comanche Native Americans in Texas. See p. 24.

Sept. 21, 1989 - Tampa City Council renamed Buffalo Avenue to Martin Luther King, Jr. Boulevard.

Sept. 25, 1911 - William H. Gray, the man who would become the fifth president of what would become Florida A&M University, was born in Richmond, Virginia.

Sept. 29, 1970 - Gwendolyn Sawyer Cherry was elected to the Florida House from Dade County and thus became the first African American woman ever to serve in the Florida Legislature.

OCTOBER

Paving roads by hand, Polk County, 1920s   Florida State Archives

Oct. 1, 1981 - Judge Joseph W. Hatchett was appointed a U.S. Circuit Judge of the United States Court of Appeals.

Oct. 3 - (1) In 1856, T. Thomas Fortune, distinguished journalist, was born in Marianna, Florida. See p. 48. (2) In 1887, the Florida state legislature established in Tallahassee the State Normal College for Colored Students, the predecessor of Florida A&M University; (3) Mary McLeod Bethune founded a school in 1904 that became Bethune-Cookman College in Daytona Beach.

Oct. 6, 1992 - Theresa Frederick was named chief of staff for the Florida House in Tallahassee, the first African American woman to hold that post.

Oct. 13, 1961 - Clifford Chester Sims of Port St. Joe, Florida, entered military service in Jacksonville on this day. He later died in the Vietnam War while saving the lives of the soldiers in his squad, for which he received the Medal of Honor. See p. 116.

Oct. 19, 1955 - The Florida Supreme Court ruled that the University of Florida could not deny admission to a person based solely on race.

Oct. 20, 1988 - The Florida Supreme Court made Virgil D. Hawkins the first attorney to be reinstated to the Florida Bar posthumously. He had been denied admission to the University of Florida law school in 1949, but had fought for many years to have other African Americans admitted to law schools in the state.

Oct. 21, 1831 - Jonathan Gibbs, who would become Florida's Superintendent of Public Instruction, was born in Philadelphia, Pennsylvania; see pp. 44-45.

Oct. 25, 1990 - Two distinguished journalists in Miami, Marc "Marcus" Garcia and Elsie Etheart, became the first Haitian journalists to win the prestigious Maria Moors Cabot Prize for the newspaper they publish: *Haiti En March*.

Oct. 31, 1948 - Baseball player Mickey Rivers was born in Miami.

Florida State Archives

NOVEMBER

Nov. 2 - (1) In **1920**, whites attacked African Americans trying to vote in Ocoee, Florida. (2) In **1992**, Carrie Meek, Corrine Brown and Alcee Hastings became the first African Americans elected to Congress from Florida since Reconstruction 125 years ago.

Nov. 4, 1950 - George William Gore, Jr., became the sixth president of Florida A&M College in Tallahassee.

Nov. 5 - (1) In **1927**, Christina Meacham, Tampa's first African American woman principal and a founder of the Hillsborough County branch of the African American teachers' organization, died in Tampa. See pp. 37-38. (2) In **1968**, Joe Lang Kershaw became the first African American since 1889 elected to serve in the Florida Legislature.

Nov. 6 - (1) In **1868**, Jonathan Gibbs began serving as Florida's Secretary of State. See p. 44. (2) In **1992**, Governor Chiles chose Carrie Meek of Miami for the Florida Women's Hall of Fame.

Nov. 8, 1870 - Josiah Walls was elected to the U.S. House of Representatives. See p. 43.

Nov. 10, 1951 - Hosea Richardson became the first African American jockey to ride in a Florida race.

Nov. 11, 1900 - Howard Thurman was born in Daytona Beach, Florida.

Nov. 13, 1985 - Dwight Gooden of Tampa became the youngest pitcher at 20 to win the Cy Young Award.

Nov. 14, 1979 - President Jimmy Carter appointed Alcee L. Hastings of Fort Lauderdale Florida's first African American Federal District Court Judge.

Nov. 15, 1873 - Florida Memorial College was incorporated as the Baptist Theological and Literary Institute in Live Oak, Florida.

Nov. 16, 1964 - Dwight Gooden, who became a pitcher for the New York Mets, was born in Tampa.

Nov. 17, 1977 - The Black Archives, History and Research Foundation of South Florida was incorporated.

Nov. 23, 1917 - The first masonry structure of Jacksonville's Stanton High School was dedicated.

Nov. 27, 1950 - Althea Gibson, the great tennis player at Florida A&M College, received the Harlem Branch (New York) YMCA Award for being the Outstanding Athlete of the Year.

Nov. 30 - (1) In **1982**, Florida's first legislative black caucus elected Sen. Carrie Meek, Miami, chairperson. (2) In **1992**, Governor Lawton Chiles appointed attorney Julia Johnson to serve on the state Public Service Commission; she was the first African American woman to serve on that commission, which regulates utilities in the state.

DECEMBER

Washerwomen, Jefferson County, Florida, circa 1870
Florida State Archives

Dec. 2 - (1) In **1933**, Florida A&M defeated Howard University, 9-6, in the first annual Orange Blossom Classic football game in Jacksonville, Florida. (2) In **1974**, the Mary McLeod Bethune Home on the campus of Bethune-Cookman College in Daytona Beach was proclaimed a National Historic Landmark.

Dec. 4, 1765 - Zephaniah Kingsley, the slave owner who owned the Kingsley Plantation above Jacksonville, was born in Scotland. See p. 17.

Dec. 5, 1935 - Mary McLeod Bethune of Daytona Beach founded the National Council of Negro Women.

Dec. 10, 1950 - The $2,000,000 Florida A&M College Hospital, Health Center and Nursing School was opened in Tallahassee.

Dec. 12, 1900 - James Weldon Johnson and J. Rosamond Johnson of Jacksonville composed "Lift Ev'ry Voice and Sing," the National Black Anthem.

Dec. 17, 1981 - Leah Alice Simms, who was elected a Dade County judge, became the first African American woman to hold a judgeship in Florida.

Dec. 19, 1889 - F. S. Fessenden, a visitor to Ocala, Florida, from Boston, provided money for establishment of an African American school, which became Fessenden Academy.

Dec. 20, 1942 -Robert "Bob" Hayes, the "world's fastest human," was born in Jacksonville.

Dec. 25, 1951 - Harry T. Moore, head of Florida's NAACP, was killed on Christmas night.

Dec. 26, 1935 - Frederick S. Humphries, who became president of Florida A&M University in Tallahassee in 1985, was born in Apalachicola, Florida.

Dec. 30, 1842 - Congressman Josiah T. Walls was born of free parents in Winchester, Virginia. He was the first African American congressman elected from the state of Florida. See pp. 42-43.

Florida A&M University

Florida Black Heritage Trail

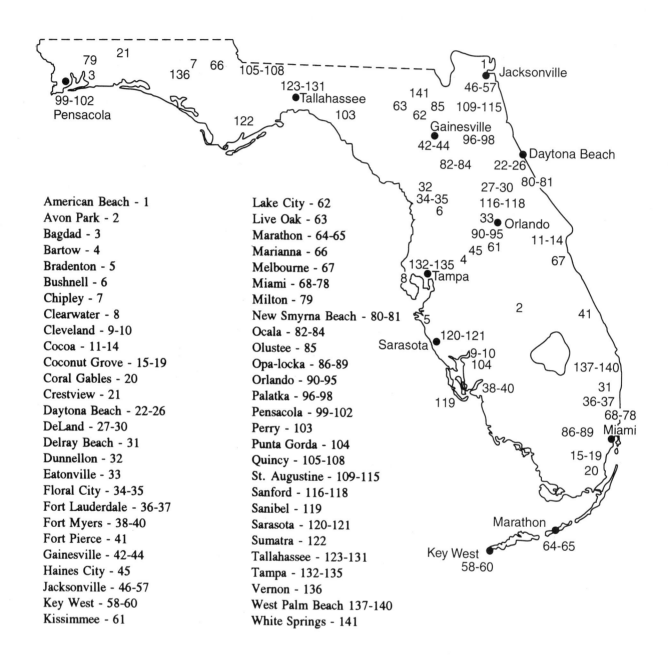

American Beach - 1
Avon Park - 2
Bagdad - 3
Bartow - 4
Bradenton - 5
Bushnell - 6
Chipley - 7
Clearwater - 8
Cleveland - 9-10
Cocoa - 11-14
Coconut Grove - 15-19
Coral Gables - 20
Crestview - 21
Daytona Beach - 22-26
DeLand - 27-30
Delray Beach - 31
Dunnellon - 32
Eatonville - 33
Floral City - 34-35
Fort Lauderdale - 36-37
Fort Myers - 38-40
Fort Pierce - 41
Gainesville - 42-44
Haines City - 45
Jacksonville - 46-57
Key West - 58-60
Kissimmee - 61

Lake City - 62
Live Oak - 63
Marathon - 64-65
Marianna - 66
Melbourne - 67
Miami - 68-78
Milton - 79
New Smyrna Beach - 80-81
Ocala - 82-84
Olustee - 85
Opa-locka - 86-89
Orlando - 90-95
Palatka - 96-98
Pensacola - 99-102
Perry - 103
Punta Gorda - 104
Quincy - 105-108
St. Augustine - 109-115
Sanford - 116-118
Sanibel - 119
Sarasota - 120-121
Sumatra - 122
Tallahassee - 123-131
Tampa - 132-135
Vernon - 136
West Palm Beach 137-140
White Springs - 141

FLORIDA BLACK HERITAGE TRAIL

American Beach
Kevin M. McCarthy

IN 1990, THE FLORIDA LEGISLATURE established a Study Commission on African American History in Florida. Two years later that Commission published a booklet called *Florida Black Heritage Trail* that listed and described 141 sites around the state that are of importance in the history of African Americans in Florida. Included below is that list of 141 places with a description of each:

1. American Beach (Nassau County)
This 50-acre community is located eight miles south of Fernandina Beach off Highway A1A on Amelia Island. Abrams L. Lewis, founder of the Afro-American Insurance Company, established the beach in the 1930s as a place for African Americans to vacation and not be bothered by the segregation that kept African Americans away from whites-only facilities.

African American executives from Florida and Georgia owned homes and businesses in American Beach. Today American Beach is one of the few remaining coastal settlements in the United States that is primarily African American. The first park in Nassau County to be named after an African American, the I. H. Burney Park, is located at the southeast end of Burney Road one block south of Lewis Street. Open 7 A.M.-7 P.M. daily.

2. Mt. Olive A.M.E. Church (Avon Park in Highlands County)
Church members raised money to build this one-story building at 900 S. Delaney Avenue in 1940. Reverend A. M. Wadell organized the congregation of this church in 1920, one year before Highlands County was established.

151

3. **New Providence Missionary Baptist Church** (Bagdad in Santa Rosa County), at 4512 Church Street, is one of the oldest churches in the county. Sons of the pastor, Rev. John Kelker, Sr., built the original church. The current structure, a wood-frame building constructed in 1901, was moved to its present location in 1989. The building will become a community center and museum about the history of the town, the churches, and the African American community.

4. **Brown Home** (Bartow in Polk County), at 470 South Second Avenue, is a private residence. In 1884, Lawrence Bernard Brown built this Victorian-style building, the oldest African American residence in town.

5. **Manatee Family Heritage House** (Bradenton in Manatee County), at 1707 15th Street East, has books, newspapers, magazines, photographs, and audiocassettes dealing with the history of African Americans in the area. Open 2 P.M. to 7 P.M., Tuesday, Wednesday, and Thursday.

6. **Dade Battlefield State Historic Site** (Bushnell in Sumter County), near U.S. 301, is the site of the 1835 battle which began the Second Seminole War, the longest and most expensive Native American war in our history. Louis Pacheco (also known as Louis Fatio), an African American slave and interpreter for Major Francis L. Dade, was one of four survivors of the Dade Massacre. The park is dedicated to the soldiers who died here. Open 9 A.M. to 5 P.M., Thursday-Monday.

7. **Roulhac Middle School** (Chipley in Washington County), at 101 North Pecan Street, was named for Orange Hill's distinguished African American educator, T. J. Roulhac, who became supervisor of Washington County's schools for African American children in 1913 and was involved in the teaching field for 49 years. All of his 10 children

also became educators. In 1938, he became principal of Chipley's first high school for African American children.

8. **Dorothy Thompson African American Museum** (Clearwater in Pinellas County), at 1501 Madison Avenue North, has over 5,000 books by African American authors, over 3,000 records and tapes, and art, newspapers, and artifacts from the first 75 families of African descent who settled in Clearwater. Phone (813) 447-1037 for appointment.

9. **Brown House** (Cleveland in Charlotte County), at 27430 Cleveland Avenue, is a private residence that used to be the home of boat-builder George Brown and his wife, Tommie. Brown built the first shipyard in the area and was active in church and city matters. He built a large, two-story house in Cleveland and hoped to have his family live there in peace and quiet, but it was not to be. He heard that other people in the town were complaining that the town's only African American would have the largest home. Not wishing to cause bad feelings among his neighbors, he sold the house to a white family and built a smaller residence for himself.

10. **Cleveland Steam Marine Ways** (also in Cleveland in Charlotte County), at 5400 Riverside Drive, is today the recreation hall for a mobile home park. It used to be the place where African American boat-builder George Brown (mentioned above) in the late 1890s built luxury yachts and repaired all kinds of boats, including sailboats and paddle-wheelers. Brown, who hired both whites and blacks, paid equal wages for equal skills. He was more concerned about how his workers did their job, than what the color of their skin was.

11. **Harry T. Moore Center** (Cocoa in Brevard County), at 307 Avocado Avenue, is a single-story building constructed in 1924 which is

used as a child-care facility and community center. Located here was the first African American school in Cocoa. The Center honors Harry Tyson Moore (1906-1951), a civil rights activist who spent much of his career with the National Association for the Advancement of Colored People (NAACP). He spent the last 17 years of his life traveling throughout Florida, organizing NAACP groups, investigating lynchings, and helping people to register to vote. On Christmas eve, 1951, a bomb exploded under his house in Mims, Florida, killing Moore and his wife Harriett; authorities have never found the person responsible for that crime.
(See pp. 106-7)

12. **Malissa Moore Home** (also in Cocoa), at 215 Stone Street, is a private residence. Workers first built this home near the Native American River in 1890 and later moved it to its current location. It has served as a restaurant and also a place where travelers could rent rooms for the night. Ms. Moore raised money to build the Mt. Moriah A.M.E. Church through Saturday-night socials and donations of 50 or 75 cents.

13. **Mt. Moriah A.M.E. Church** (also in Cocoa), at 304 Stone Street, was built in 1923. In 1922, fire destroyed the original church building, but Malissa Moore, a founding member of the church, once again raised funds to rebuild the church.

14. **Richard E. Stone Historic District** (also in Cocoa), at 121-304 Stone Street, honors Richard E. Stone, the inventor of a directional signal light for automobiles in 1935. He also helped start the Cocoa-Rockledge Civic League.

15. **Black Heritage Museum** (Coconut Grove in Dade County), at 3301 Coral Way in the Miracle Center Mall, has a permanent collection of tribal artifacts from the west coast of Africa and New Guinea, as well as a large collection of black Americana. Open 11 A.M.-4 P.M. Monday-Friday; 1 PM-4 PM weekends/holidays. Phone: (305) 446-7304 or (305) 252-3535.

16. **Charles Avenue Historic District** (Coconut Grove), which is indicated by a marker at Charles Avenue and Main Highway, is the site of the first black community on the south Florida mainland. It began here in the late 1880s when blacks, who came mostly from the Bahamas, arrived by way of Key West to work at the Peacock Inn, the first hotel in the Miami area. Their knowledge of tropical plants and building materials helped them develop Coconut Grove.

17. **Coconut Grove Cemetery** (Coconut Grove), near 3650 Charles Avenue, was developed in 1913 by the Coconut Grove Colored Cemetery Association, whose members included some of the most important African American citizens of Coconut Grove, for example E.W.F. Stirrup, Walker Burrows, and Joseph Riddick. Many influential pioneer settlers of the area are buried in this cemetery.

18. **Macedonia Baptist Church** (Coconut Grove), at 3315 Douglas Road, was the site of Dade County's first Baptist church for African Americans. It began in 1895 and was called the Fifty-Six Baptist Church because it had 56 charter members. In 1903, the congregation built the first church building on Charles Avenue and changed its name to St. Agnes Missionary Baptist Church. In 1922, they changed the name to Macedonia Baptist Church. Workers completed the present structure in 1948. In 1993, officials dedicated several historical markers there to commemorate the many contributions that Bahamian and African American pioneers made to the area.

19. **Stirrup House** (Coconut Grove), at 3242 Charles Avenue, is a private residence. In 1897,

Ebenezer W. F. Stirrup, a native of the Bahamas who had come to the United States in 1888, built this two-story structure of tough Florida pine. Stirrup, who was Dade County's first African American millionaire, built over 100 homes to rent or sell to other Bahamian blacks who came to Coconut Grove around 1900. Descendants of some of those early pioneers still live in some of those houses.

20. **MacFarlane Homestead Subdivision Historic District** (Coral Gables in Dade County) is bordered by Oak Avenue, Grand Avenue, Brooker Street and Jefferson Street. It has homes built in the late 1920s and 1930s in an unusual architectural style not seen elsewhere in Coral Gables. Some of the houses are bungalows and one-story "shotgun" houses. St. Mary's Baptist Church at 136 Frow Avenue was built in 1927.

21. **Carver-Hill Memorial Museum** (Crestview in Okaloosa County) is in Fairview Park in the 900 block of McClelland Street. This building was constructed in 1942 as a military barracks, but now is a museum that preserves African American culture and the achievements of the African Americans of Crestview. Phone: (904) 682-3494.

22. **Mary McLeod Bethune House** (Daytona Beach in Volusia County), at 641 Pearl Street off Second Avenue, is a simple two-story vernacular building where Mary McLeod Bethune lived from the time of its construction in the 1920s until she died in 1955. The building houses a museum containing original furnishings and archives for the Mary McLeod Bethune papers. Open Monday-Friday; tours upon request. Phone: (904) 255-1401, extension 372. For more about her see pp. 60-63.

Mary McLeod Bethune leaving White Hall at Bethune-Cookman College.

23. **Bethune-Cookman College** (Daytona Beach), at 640 Second Avenue, is the school that Mary McLeod Bethune established in 1904, first as the Daytona Educational and Industrial Training School for Negro Girls. In 1923, she joined her school with Jacksonville's all-male Cookman Institute to form Bethune-Cookman Institute, now known as Bethune-Cookman College.

24. **Museum of Arts and Sciences** (Daytona Beach), at 1040 Museum Boulevard, includes a section filled with artifacts dealing with the African cultural history of African Americans. Its African art collection is one of the best in the Southeast. Open 9 A.M.-4 P.M., Tuesday-Friday; 12 noon-5 P.M. on weekends.

25. **Jackie Robinson Memorial Ball Park** (Daytona Beach) on City Island. On March 17, 1946, in Daytona Beach, the great baseball player, Jackie Robinson, played his first game as a member of the Brooklyn Dodgers minor-league team. That game was the first integrated game in professional baseball. In 1947, Robinson joined the Brooklyn Dodgers and made baseball history as the first African American player in the major leagues. In September 1990 officials dedicated a commemorative statue by Montreal sculptor Jules LaSalle.

26. **Howard Thurman House** (Daytona Beach), at 614 Whitehall Street, was the childhood home of Howard Thurman (1900-1981). *Ebony* magazine called this great minister and theologian one of the 50 most important figures in African American history; *Life* magazine called him one of the 12 best preachers in the nation. Built around 1888 in one of the oldest residential sections of Daytona Beach, the two-story building was Thurman's home from his birth to his departure for a Jacksonville high school in 1917. Throughout his life he often returned to visit his childhood home.

27. **Bradley Hall** – Safe Home Orphanage– (DeLand in Volusia County), at 511 S. Clara Avenue, is a private residence that was built in 1925 as an orphanage for African American children.

28. **Old DeLand Colored Hospital** (DeLand) on Stone Street is important in the history of medical services for African Americans in Volusia County. If one contrasts this plain building, which was built in 1926, with the Old DeLand Memorial Hospital for whites, one can see how different public facilities were during the 1920s, when segregation was in effect.

29. **J.W. Wright Building** (DeLand), at 258-264 W. Voorhis Avenue in the Yemassee settlement (see below). The two-story structure, which architect Francis Miller designed, was built in 1920 for $15,000. Miller also designed Old DeLand Memorial Hospital, a facility for whites mentioned in #28 above.

Howard Thurman
Florida Satte Archives

30. **Yemassee Settlement** (DeLand), in the area around Voorhis, Euclid, Adelle, and Clara Avenues, was an exclusive black settlement in the early part of this century. The area has some of the oldest buildings associated with African American residential neighborhoods in DeLand. One good example of such a building is the Greater Union Baptist Church, which was built at 240 South Clara Avenue in 1893.

31. **B. F. James & Frances Jane Bright Mini-Park** (Delray Beach in Palm Beach County) is on the east side of N.W. 5th Avenue, 100 feet south of N.W. 1st Street. A bronze marker there mentions five historic places in one of the oldest sections of Delray Beach, places that played an important role in the early development of the town: School No. 4 Delray Colored, located at the site; Greater Mount Olive Missionary Baptist Church at 40 N.W. 4th Avenue; St. Paul A.M.E. Church at 119 N.W. 5th Avenue; Free and Accepted Masons, Lodge 275, at 85 N.W. 5th Avenue; and St. Matthew Episcopal Church at 404 S.W. 3rd Street.

32. **Second Bethel Baptist Church** (Dunnellon in Marion County) and its Annie Johnson Center, east of U.S. Highway 41, south of Dunnellon in Citrus County. This building, which serves today as a Human Resource Center, was finished in 1888 and was a school for the African American community. Pastor Henry Shaw was the first to minister to African Americans who worked in the turpentine, sawmill, and phosphate industries in the area.

33. **Eatonville** (in Orange County) off U.S. 17-92 north of Orlando between Winter Park and Maitland. This was the home of famed author Zora Neale Hurston (1891?-1960) and the country's oldest African American town, incorporated in 1887. A marker in the Zora Neale Hurston Memorial Park at 11 People Street in the Eatonville Municipal Complex

Eatonville: Zora Neale Hurston plaque
Kevin M. McCarthy

honors this great American writer, as does the annual "ZORA!" festival. See pp. 78-80.

34. **Frasier Cemetery** (Floral City in Citrus County), on the corner of Great Oaks Drive and East Tower Trail, is an African American cemetery established in 1908 by H. C. Frasier when he buried his son there. Many of the early workers in the phosphate mines were African Americans and are buried in this cemetery.

35. **Pleasant Hill Baptist Church** (Floral City) at 8200 E. Magnolia Street is the oldest religious building for African Americans in Floral City. The church was built between 1895 and 1910.

36. **Old Dillard High School** (Fort Lauderdale in Broward County), at 1001 N.W. 4th Street, is one of the oldest buildings in the city, having been built in 1924. This school, which was called the "Colored School," was the first school for African Americans in Fort Lauderdale. Among the many good teachers who taught there was jazz musician Cannonball Adderley, who taught music there for two years. The building has a museum dedicated to Clarence C. Walker, a principal who worked hard to keep the high school open for nine months. Up until 1942, African American schools were closed from November until March so the children could work in

156

the fields and help pick green beans and peppers. He convinced many people that it was more important for the children to be in school than to be in the fields.

37. Dr. James F. Sistrunk Boulevard Historical Marker (Fort Lauderdale), at 1400 block, Sistrunk Blvd., N.W. 6th Street, is dedicated to a doctor who began practicing medicine in the area in 1921. Dr. Sistrunk (1891-1966) made house calls to poor neighborhoods and often did not charge anything for his services. For 16 years this man, whom the people called "Old Doc," was the only physician in the city's African American community. In 1938, he and Dr. Von Delaney Mizell established Provident Hospital, Fort Lauderdale's first African American hospital. Dr. Sistrunk kept practicing medicine and delivering babies until he died of cancer on March 20, 1966.

38. Paul Laurence Dunbar School (Fort Myers in Lee County), at 1857 High Street, was finished in 1927 and served as the high school for the predominantly African American Dunbar community and the surrounding area. Before September 1925, African Americans could attend only grades 1-6. The building now houses adult education classes and other community services. Williams Academy, which served as the African American school until Dunbar School opened, has been moved here.

39. McCullum Hall (Fort Myers), on the northeast corner of Cranford and Dr. Martin Luther King, Jr., Boulevard, was an entertainment spot for the African American community as well as the USO for African American World War II soldiers training at Page and Buckingham Fields. Famous entertainers like Duke Ellington and Count Basie appeared here. Built around 1938, the building is now a store and rooming house.

40. Etta Powell Home (Fort Myers), at 2764 Lime Street, is now a private residence but use to be one of the homes where African American major league baseball players stayed when their teams were training at Terry Park; they were not allowed in area hotels. Baseball players last used the Etta Powell Home in 1970.

41. Zora Neale Hurston House (Fort Pierce in St. Lucie County), at 1734 School Court Street, is now a private residence. This simple one-story concrete-block house, with its small 28-foot-square area, is the house in which Hurston lived and worked. She paid a local physician $10 a week rent, but he reduced this to nothing when she was out of work. Hurston, who moved to Fort Pierce in 1957, lived here while she worked as a reporter for *The Fort Pierce Chronicle* and while she was writing a book about Herod the Great. When Hurston died in 1960, she was buried in an unmarked grave in a cemetery on 17th Street:

Fort Pierce: Zora Neale Hurston house
Kevin M. McCarthy

had a gravestone put on the site; the stone reads

Zora Neale Hurston
"A Genius of the South"
1901-1960
Novelist, Folklorist
Anthropologist

42. Mt. Pleasant A.M.E. Church (Gainesville in Alachua County), at 630 N.W. 2nd Street, was built in 1906 after fire destroyed the original wooden church that had been built in 1884. The congregation was organized in 1867. Some consider this building, which is the oldest African American church in Gainesville, the most important building in the Pleasant Street Historic District from an architectural standpoint.

43. Pleasant Street Historic District (Gainesville) is the oldest and largest continuously inhabited African American residential area in Gainesville. The district was the religious and social center for African American entertainment, commerce, education, and church life in the city. The African Americans who settled in the district and built the 255 historic buildings here were skilled blacksmiths, shoemakers, carpenters, and tailors who found work in town. In 1867, two years after the end of the Civil War, local people bought land for two important institutions in the neighborhood: the church and the Union Academy. The Academy, which the Freedmen's Bureau established in 1867 and which had 179 students the following year, remained the central African American educational institution until 1925, at which time it became a recreation center.

44. Josiah Walls Historical Marker (Gainesville), on University Avenue between 1st and 2nd Streets, honors the first African American United States Congressman elected from Florida. Josiah Walls (1842-1905) served as a soldier for the Union in the Civil War, owned a newspaper in Gainesville, served as

mayor of Gainesville, was Florida's only congressman in the House of Representatives in Washington, and was the last African American representing Florida until the November 1992 election. See pp. 42-43.

45. Bethune Neighborhood Center (Haines City in Polk County), at 8th Street and Avenue E, used to be known as Oakland High School. These five buildings made up a school for African American children from Haines City, Loughman, Davenport, Lake Hamilton, Dundee, and the unincorporated areas of Northeast Polk County. It is now used for civic, recreational, and educational functions.

46. Bethel Baptist Institutional Church (Jacksonville in Duval County), at 1058 North Hogan Street, has served as the center of the religious and community life of Jacksonville's African American citizens since it was built in 1904. The congregation was first organized in July 1838 with six charter members, including two slaves, under the leadership of its first pastor, James McDonald. In 1840, the members of the church bought property at the northeast corner of Duval and Newnan Streets, where they built Bethel Baptist Church, the first church building in Jacksonville. When the Civil War ended, some members wanted to separate the white and African American members of the congregation. In an 1868 agreement, the African American members withdrew to build a new church, keeping the Bethel Baptist name. After the 1901 fire destroyed the church building, church officials had a new church built with a beautiful bell tower that dominates the neighborhood.

47. Catherine Street Fire Station #3 (Jacksonville) at 12 Catherine Street was built in 1902 to replace a station destroyed by the Great Jacksonville Fire of 1901. African American firemen manned the station for several years. Officials made plans to tear down the

Bethel Baptist Institutional Church
Florida State Archives

building in 1972 to provide room for the new Police Administration Building, but, when those officials learned of the building's significance, they built the new building around the fire station. It now serves as the museum of the city's fire-fighting history. Notice the large, arched door to accommodate horse-drawn fire wagons. Officials may move the fire station to a location in Metropolitan Park approximately 1/4 mile to the east. Tours are available by appointment. Phone: (904)630-2453.

48. **Centennial Hall** (Jacksonville) at 1715 Kings Road was named to commemorate the centennial (100th anniversary) of the African Methodist Episcopal Church. The Rev. Richard L. Brown (1854-1948), Jacksonville's first African American architect, built this three-story brick structure in 1916 although he had had no formal training in architecture. The building cost $30,000 to build and had a small, eight-sided cupola on the roof, which was re-moved when the building was changed to become the library for Edward Waters College. See pp. 46-47 for more about the college.

49. **Kingsley Plantation State Historic Site,** at 11676 Palmetto Avenue on Fort George Island off Highway A1A, is one of the few remaining examples of the plantation system of territorial Florida and is the site of the oldest plantation house in the state. Although Zephaniah Kingsley was married to an African woman and wanted slaves to be treated well, he believed that slavery was necessary for the success of agriculture in the South. One can visit the 1817 house and the slave cabins. Open 8 A.M.-sunset, daily. There are guided tours Thursday-Monday. Phone: (904) 251-3122. See pp. 17-19.

50. **Masonic Temple Building** (Jacksonville) at 410 Broad Street, which was built in 1912 by the Black Masons of Florida, serves as the

headquarters of the Masons of the State of Florida Grand East. The red-brick structure serves the African American community's commercial and fraternal activities, with retail on the first floor, offices on the second and third floors, and the Masonic organization on the fourth and fifth floors. In its early days, African American doctors, dentists, insurance agents, and other professionals had offices here. Jacksonville's first African American-owned bank, the Anderson Bank, was also located here. The 1926 *Negro Blue Book* described the structure as "one of the finest buildings owned by Negroes in the world."

51. Mount Olive A.M.E. Church (Jacksonville) at 841 Franklin Street has an unusual style that combines different elements. Richard L. Brown, Jacksonville's first African American architect, designed the 1921-22 church and used concrete block and brown mortar to add a rich color tone. Workers made the concrete blocks look like quarry stone on the top two stories.

52. Mount Zion A.M.E. Church (Jacksonville) at 201 East Beaver Street has beautiful arched windows and door openings, stained-glass windows, and a large bell tower. After the Civil War, a group of freedmen came together for religious worship and became formally recognized as the Mount Zion A.M.E. Church on July 28, 1866. Members bought the property at the northeast corner of Newnan and Beaver Streets and built a small house of worship. They built a large wooden church in 1870 and, 20 years later, an even larger brick building for 1500 members. Four months after the great 1901 fire destroyed their brick building, members were planning their new building, which would cost about $18,000. The bell tower is still a handsome landmark in the area.

53. Old Brewster Hospital (Jacksonville), at 915 West Monroe Street, is now a private residence that was built in 1885 and still has its famous "gingerbread" porches and the numerals 1885 cut into the top of the columns. In 1901 the Women's Home Missionary Society of the Methodist Church bought the building and, with a gift of $1500 from Mrs. George A. Brewster, established a hospital and nurse-training facility which was the first Jacksonville hospital for African Americans. The hospital moved to other facilities in 1910, but the original building still stands. Brewster Hospital closed in 1966, after the 1964 Civil Rights Act opened the city's other hospitals to African Americans and therefore led to a loss of income for Brewster Hospital.

Kingsley Plantation
Kevin M. McCarthy

54. Ritz Theater (Jacksonville), at 825 Davis Street in a traditionally African American commercial district in the La Villa neighborhood, presents a combination of Egyptian, Mediterranean, and Art Deco styles. Local architect Jefferson Powell designed the building, which included a cinema, shops, and offices. The Ritz, which opened in September 1929, served the surrounding African American community for almost 30 years. The building is now vacant and in poor condition, but it may be restored to help bring new life to the area.

55. Stanton High School (Jacksonville) at 521 W. Ashley Street was established in 1868 as the first public school for African American children in Jacksonville. When Ossian Hart, the son of Jacksonville's founder and the tenth governor of Florida, sold the land to the school's officials, he insisted that the land be used only for educational purposes. The school's name

Stanton High School
P. K. Yonge Library of Florida History, University of Florida

honors Edwin M. Stanton, an abolitionist and Secretary of War under President Abraham Lincoln. In its first year of operation the school had six teachers and 348 students. When the building was finished in 1917, it was the only high school for African Americans in Duval County. James Weldon Johnson was a student at Stanton High and served as principal from 1894 to 1902. For more about him see pp. 75-77. The old school building, which closed in 1971, may become a community center, a memorial to the long struggle for equal education. The school itself continues as the Stanton College Preparatory High School.

56. Edward Waters College (Jacksonville) at 1658 Kings Road is the oldest school established for the education of African Americans in Florida. The African Methodist Episcopal Church established the original school in 1866, right after the American Civil War. Teachers from New England were coming south to teach former slaves wherever they could find a classroom; for example, they taught in church basements, box cars, jails, and old buildings. Three years after fire destroyed the original school in 1901, officials moved the college to Kings Road. Among its many graduates were Asa Philip Randolph, national leader in the black labor movement. See pp. 46-47 for more about the college.

57. Clara White Mission (Jacksonville), at 611-13 West Ashley Street, honors the many kind acts done by Clara English White and her daughter, Eartha M. M. White, for Jacksonville's African Americans. Clara White, who belonged to the Bethel Baptist Church, served free dinners, ran soup kitchens, and gave out food to anyone who needed help. She and her daughter also collected money to build a home for the elderly. Architect H. J. Klutho designed the building, which continues to serve the Jacksonville community. See pp. 72-74 for more about Clara White and her daughter.

58. **Bahama Village** (Key West in Monroe County) is a 12-block area surrounded by Whitehead, Louisa, Fort, and Angela streets; it is the chief African American residential area of Key West. Persons of African descent who had arrived from the U.S. mainland, the Bahamas, and the Caribbean began settling here in the mid-1800s. Some of them came looking for freedom; others came looking for work in the sponge and turtle industries. Most of the neighborhood houses were built before 1912 with historic churches scattered among them. Some of the street names honor the early settlers from the Bahamas. Among the important African Americans who had homes in the area were Robert Gabriel (Monroe County's representative in the state legislature in 1879) and Mildred Shaver (principal of the Frederick Douglass School in the early 20th century).

59. **Cornish Memorial A.M.E. Zion Church** (Key West) at 702 Whitehead Street, which was built in 1903, honors Sandy Cornish, an early immigrant from the Bahamas who founded the congregation in 1865.

60. **Nelson English Park** (Key West), on the corner of Thomas and Amelia Streets in Bahama Village, is named for the African American civic leader who was the postmaster in Key West from 1882 to 1886.

61. **Bethel A.M.E. Church** (Kissimmee in Osceola County), at 1702 North Brack Street, is a one-story building that was built in 1916. The cornerstone mentions the name of Lawrence Silas, a prosperous African American cattleman in Florida's range country who owned thousands of head of cattle. Florida's great African American writer, Zora Neale Hurston, wrote about Silas in *The Saturday Evening Post* (Sept. 5, 1942, pp. 18, 55-57). (See also #80 below.)

62. **Florida Sports Hall of Fame** (Lake City in Columbia County), at 601 Hall of Fame Drive, 1/4 mile north of U.S. 90 and 1/2 mile west of Interstate 75, was founded in 1958 as a showcase for Florida's sports heroes. Exhibits and video displays highlight the careers of some of Florida's great African American sports figures like baseball stars Andre Dawson, Hal McRae, and Tim Raines, football stars like Wes Chandler, Alonzo S. "Jake" Gaither, Bob Hayes, and Paul Warfield, and tennis star Althea Gibson. Open 9 A.M.-9 P.M., Monday-Saturday, 10 A.M. - 7 P.M., Sunday.

Lake City: Florida Sports Hall of Fame
Kevin M. McCarthy

63. African Missionary Baptist Church (Live Oak in Suwannee County) at 509 Walker Avenue S.W., two blocks south of Highway 90, was built in 1910. Ms. Nancy Parshley, a wealthy, kind white woman, donated the land on the corner of Parshley and Houston Avenue where the first church was built.

64. Adderly House (Marathon in Monroe County) at 5550 Overseas Highway is now a private residence. It was built around 1906 by George Adderly, a black immigrant from the Bahamas who worked as a sponger, boatman, and charcoal maker. The one-story building, which has an unusual hip roof similar to residences built by blacks in the Bahamas during the 19th century, is today part of the Crane Point Historic and Archaeological District.

65. Pigeon Key Historic District (Marathon), off U.S. Highway 1 at mile marker 45, consists of seven buildings built between 1909 and 1920 as a camp for workers building Henry Flagler's railroad to Key West, the one that many people called the "overseas railroad." The camp includes a 1912 "Negro Workers' Cottage" which housed African Americans during the period. The site will become a recreational facility to include displays about the history of the railroad.

66. Joseph W. Russ, Jr. House (Marianna in Jackson County), at 310 W. Lafayette Street, is now a private residence, but used to be the main plantation house near the birthplace of T. Thomas Fortune (1856-1928). This former slave left Florida and became a famous newspaper writer in New York City. Before leaving Marianna, he worked for the local newspaper, the *Marianna Courier*, and liked it so much that he later went to Jacksonville and worked on a newspaper there. As an adult, he helped establish the National Afro-American League. He spent a good part of his adult life fighting for equal rights for all African Americans. For more about him see pp. 48-49.

67. Wright Brothers House (Melbourne in Brevard County), at 2310 1/2 Lipscomb Street, is now a private residence that was built around 1892. Wright Brothers was among the first settlers of Melbourne, establishing his homestead in the area by 1877.

68. Bill Baggs Cape Florida State Recreation Area (Miami in Dade County), on Key Biscayne east of Miami, was the place where many black Seminoles and escaped slaves set off in boats for the Bahamas when the United States took control of Florida from Spain in 1821. When angry Native Americans attacked the Cape Florida Lighthouse on July 23, 1836, the lighthouse keeper and his assistant, an African American by the name of Henry, fled to the lighthouse, but not before the Native Americans wounded them with bullets. Henry soon died; the lighthouse keeper was later rescued. Visitors today can tour the grounds and go through the lighthouse keeper's house. Open 8 a.m.-sunset, year-round. See pp. 20-21.

69. Black Archives, History and Research Foundation of South Florida (Miami) in the Joseph Caleb Community Center, 5400 N.W. 22nd Avenue, Suite 702, houses many manuscripts and photographs about African American history in Dade County. Among the art pieces is a portrait of African American artist Joseph Caleb, for whom the center is named. Open 1 P.M.-5 P.M., daily. Research hours by appointment. Phone: (305) 636-2390.

70. Chapman House (Miami), at 1200 N.W. 6th Avenue, was built in 1923 by Dr. William A. Chapman, Sr. He was the first-known African American expert that the State Board of Health hired in its efforts to control disease in the area. The City of Miami declared the site a historic site in 1983 and ten years later established The Chapman House Ethnic Heritage Children's Folklife Educational Center there. The Center was to emphasize Miami's diverse cultural influences. The new Booker T. Washington High School (see #78) is on the grounds there.

71. **Greater Bethel A.M.E. Church** (Miami), at 245 N.W. 8th Street, was organized in 1896, several months before the city was incorporated. Construction of the building began in 1927, but was not completed until 1942. This building is one of the few examples of the Mediterranean Revival architectural style in Overtown (see #75, below).

72. **Florida Memorial College** (Miami), at 15800 N.W. 42nd Ave (LeJeune Road), was formed from two colleges in north Florida. In the late 1800s, the American Baptist Home Mission Society established two colleges: The Florida Baptist Institute for Negroes in Live Oak (1879) and the Florida Baptist Academy in Jacksonville (1892). After several name changes and relocations, the two institutions joined up in 1941 and, in 1968, moved from Saint Augustine to the present modern campus in Miami.

73. **Lincoln Memorial Park** (Miami), at N.W. 46th Street and N.W. 30th Avenue, was a cemetery which opened in 1924 and remained for many years the place where African Americans in Miami buried their dead. The funeral processions sometimes included friends and family members playing tuba and trumpet. African American pioneers buried here include Dana Albert Dorsey (Miami's first African American millionaire) and Gwendolyn Sawyer Cherry (the first African American woman to serve in the Florida legislature).

74. **Lyric Theatre** (Miami), at 819 N.W. 2nd Avenue, is a vaudeville and movie theater that African American Geder Walker built in 1915. Once one of the major centers of entertainment for African Americans, this building is the only one remaining in Overtown in the district known as "Little Broadway," which reached its peak during the 1930s and 1940s.

75. **Overtown Neighborhood** (Miami), between N.W. Second and Third Avenues and N.W. Eighth and Tenth Streets, dates from 1896. This area, one of the oldest neighborhoods in Miami and once called Colored Town, became an important location for schools, churches, and businesses. It was first settled by African Americans brought in by developer Henry Flagler, who was extending his railroad down the east coast of Florida; it would eventually reach Key West. Among the town's dozens of businesses were hotels like the Sir John, the Mary Elizabeth, and the Dorsey, where entertainers like Cab Calloway, Nat "King" Cole, and Billie Holiday stayed, as well as sports stars like Joe Louis and Jackie Robinson. Developers hope to restore the place with a regional cultural and entertainment tourist attraction that will include displays about the history of Overtown and the African Americans who lived there.

76. **St. John's Baptist Church** (Miami), at 1328 N.W. 3rd Avenue, has a congregation that was organized in 1906. In 1940, workers finished the building there which the African American architectural firm of McKissack and McKissack designed.

77. **The Vanguard—Miami's Forerunners of Human Progress** (Miami) houses the Historical Museum of Southern Florida, 111 Flagler Street. The Urban League of Greater Miami, Inc., had this mural done of Miami's African American history in honor of the 25th anniversary of the passage of the 1965 Voting Rights Act. Open 10 A.M.-5 P.M., Monday- Saturday;. 10 A.M.-9 P.M., Thursday; 12 Noon -5-P.M., Sunday.

78. **Booker T. Washington High School** (Miami), at 1200 N.W. 6th Avenue, was started in 1926 despite the objections of people living in the area. Because workers feared that some of those people might try to destroy the building, they took turns stand-

ing guard at night and working during the day, until they finished building the school. It officially opened on March 28, 1927. This was the first school in South Florida to provide a 12th-grade education for African American children. The school today serves the middle grade levels.

79. **Mount Pilgrim African Baptist Church** (Milton in Santa Rosa County), on the corner of Alice and Clara Streets, was organized in 1866 by African Americans who left the First Baptist Church. Members of the church also helped establish four other African American congregations in the community. Wallace A. Rayfield, a leading African American architect in the South in the early 20th century, designed this 1916 building.

80. **Bethune—Volusia Beach** (New Smyrna Beach in Volusia County off Highway A1A), six miles south of New Smyrna Beach, has long been a popular beach for African Americans. This ocean-front land was developed in the 1940s by such important people as educator Mary McLeod Bethune, insurance executive G. D. Rogers of Tampa, rancher Lawrence Silas of Kissimmee, and other African American investors.

81. **Old Sacred Heart/St. Rita (Colored) Mission Church** (New Smyrna Beach), at 312 N. Duss Street, was built in 1899 as a house of worship for a community of African American Roman Catholics.

82. **Fessenden Elementary School** (Ocala in Marion County), at 4200 N.W. 90th Street, was established in 1868, three years after the end of the Civil War. This school challenged African American students, most of whom had little opportunity for education in Florida. The school became Fessenden Academy in 1898 to honor Ferdinand Stone Fessenden. He was a wealthy businessman from Boston who helped pay for the school and encouraged the American Missionary Association to sponsor it. The school, which is actually in Martin near Ocala, educated African Americans from Florida and other Southern states from 1868 until 1951. Many of its graduates went on to colleges and universities and jobs of importance throughout the United States. The existing buildings date from the Depression era. Phone: (904)662-5234.

83. **Howard Academy Community Center** (Ocala), at 306 NW 7th Avenue, was established in 1885 by the Board of Public Instruc-

Booker T. Washington High School
Florida State Archives

A monument on the battlefield
Florida State Archives

tion as a school for Negroes. It now serves as a neighborhood center.

84. Mount Zion A.M.E. Church (Ocala), at 623 S. Magnolia Avenue, is the only surviving brick, 19th-century religious structure in Ocala. It stands behind the site of the original white-frame building. Construction of this first brick church owned by an African American congregation began in 1891 under the supervision of African American architect and builder Levi Alexander, Sr. The building's most prominent feature is its two-story tower.

85. Olustee Battlefield State Historic Site (Olustee in Baker County), 15 miles east of Lake City and two miles east of Olustee on U.S. Highway 90, is the place where Florida's major Civil War battle took place. On February 20, 1864, approximately 5500 Union troops, including three African American infantry regiments, were marching westward from the St. Johns River. They wanted to capture cattle, seize crops, take in more African Americans to become soldiers, and stop people from giving supplies to the Confederate soldiers. The Confederate forces met the Union troops near a place called Ocean Pond. After a battle that lasted five hours, the Union forces retreated to Jacksonville. Open 9 A.M.-5 P.M., daily. Signs along the trail point out the important facts about the battle; a visitors' center gives more information about the Confederate victory. Each February over 1,000 people dress up as Union and Confederate troops to act out the battle once again. Phone: (904)752-3866. See pp. 33-34.

86. Opa-locka Thematic Development (Opa-locka in Dade County) is located northwest of Miami. This mostly African American town is unusual because it uses the Moorish Revival architectural style. Aviation pioneer Glen H. Curtiss helped develop the town in the 1920s land boom and modeled some of the buildings on the *Arabian Nights* stories. Today, many of the original 100 buildings remain in this city, which has been called "The Bagdad of South Florida."

87. Harry Hurt Building (Opa-locka), at the corner of Ali-Baba Avenue and Opa-locka Boulevard, is one of the most distinguished buildings in this unique town. The building, built in

1926 as a shopping and service center, has retained much of its original character, including a central dome surrounded by minarets. On the second floor were apartments, a social hall, and offices. After World War II it became the Opa-locka Hotel.

88. **Opa-locka City Hall** (Opa-locka), at 777 Sharazad Boulevard, may have been designed after a place mentioned in the story "The Talk Bird." The building, which the city bought in 1939 for use as a city hall, has been restored. For several years after the death of Glen Curtiss in 1930, the aviation pioneer who developed Opa-locka, the building remained unpainted, but the city has done much to restore it to its former splendor. The large hall has murals, painted in 1926, of scenes from the *Arabian Nights*.

89. **Opa-locka Railroad Station** (Opa-locka), in the 500 block of Ali-Baba Avenue, looks like an abandoned fortress in the Arabian desert. The design of the 1927 railroad station is based on the tales "Ali Baba and the Forty Thieves" and "Aladdin and his Lamps." One can still see fine handmade tiles around the arches, doors, and windows of this building.

90. **Callahan Neighborhood** (Orlando in Orange County) is bordered by Colonial Drive, Central Avenue, Division Street, and Orange Blossom Trail. This neighborhood, started in 1886, is one of the oldest African American communities in Orlando and includes the Callahan Neighborhood Center, formerly the old Jones High School, which was established in 1985.

91. **J. A. Colyer Building** (Orlando), at 27-29 Church Street, is currently an Irish pub. This building was built in 1911 and housed the Colyer and Williams tailor shop, an African American business that was located among white businesses in downtown Orlando.

92. **Dr. I. S. Hankins House** (Orlando), at 219 Lime Street, is now a private residence. This home was built in 1935 as the home of Orlando's pioneer African American physician who encouraged improved race relations and African American home ownership.

93. **Old Ebenezer Church** (Orlando), at 596 West Church Street, was built around 1900 by members of the Ebenezer United Methodist Church. After the congregation moved, the building became home to the Greater Refuge Church of Our Lord.

94. **Old Mount Pleasant Baptist Church** (Orlando), at 701 West South Street, was built in 1920. It now houses the Tabernacle of the Enlightened Church of God.

Orlando: The Riley Building
Kevin M. McCarthy

95. **The Riley Building** (Orlando), at 571-75 West Church Street, was built in 1947 by businessman Zellie L. Riley, who operated a tailor shop and men's ready-to-wear store. Riley encouraged African American business opportunity through the Negro Chamber of Commerce.

96. **Bethel A.M.E. Church** (Palatka in Putnam County), at 719 Reid Street, was built by the congregation around 1908-1912. The residents of the nearby community of Newtown organized the church in 1866.

97. **Finley Homestead** (Palatka), at 522 Main Street, is now a private residence. This two-story building was the home of Adam Finley, a free, African American artisan who obtained the property in 1883. His grandson, Dr. Harold E. Finley, was a nationally known zoologist.

98. **Old Central Academy High School** (Palatka), at 1207 Washington Street, was established in 1892. It became the first accredited Negro high school in Florida in 1924. Fire destroyed the first Central Academy building in 1936. The building there now replaced it in 1937 and serves as the County School Board Service Center.

99. **Daniel "Chappie" James' Birthplace** (Pensacola in Escambia County), at 1606 N. Alcaniz Street, is where Chappie James was born in 1920 and where his mother, Lillie A. James, ran a school for African American children. The front steps are painted white and labeled "Chappie's First Steps." "Chappie" James became the first African American four-star general in American military history. He served his country as a fighter pilot in Korea and Vietnam. For more about him see #100 below and pp. 118-119.

100. **Julee Cottage Museum** (Pensacola), at 210 E. Zaragoza Street in the Seville Square Historic District, is a simple wood-frame building that was built between 1804 and 1808. It is one of Pensacola's oldest wooden buildings that still exists. It belonged to Julee Panton, a "free woman of color," who did well as a businesswoman in real estate. She used her money to buy slaves and then would let them earn money and work off their debt to her and thus gain their freedom. A Black History Museum tells the history of African Americans in the Florida Panhandle, for example Daniel "Chappie" James (see #99 above). Open 10 A.M. - 4:30 P.M., Monday-Saturday. Phone: (904)444-8986.

101. **Mount Zion Baptist Church** (Pensacola), at 528 West Jackson Street, was constructed in 1918. After the congregation was organized in 1880, fire twice destroyed the church buildings, but the members vowed to stay on.

102. **Saint Michael's Creole Benevolent Association Hall** (Pensacola) at 416 East Government Street in the Seville Square Historic District. Members of the St. Michael's Creole Benevolent Association built the hall in 1895 and used it over the years for youth events including boxing, meetings, dances, and receptions. The Pensacola Creoles were racially mixed from unions of Spanish and African Americans; in 1878, a Creole was elected mayor of Pensacola. When the Pensacola public schools were desegregated in 1969, the Creoles became less separated from the rest of society. The building was restored in 1972. Open 10 A.M.-4:30 P.M., Monday-Saturday. Phone: (904)444-8986.

103. **Painting entitled "Cypress Logging"** (Perry in Taylor County) in the U.S. Post Office, 1600 South Jefferson Street, shows scenes from the lumber industry in which many African Americans worked. Florida artist George Snow Hill painted this as part of a national program in which the federal government used artists to paint public buildings. Originally

hung in the Old Perry Post Office at 201 East Green Street in February 1938, the painting was moved to its present location in 1987.

104. **Baker Elementary School** (Punta Gorda in Charlotte County), at 311 East Charlotte Avenue, was named for the first principal-teacher of the county's first "colored school": Benjamin Joshua Baker. Dan T. Smith, the first African American appointed to the DeSoto County Board of Education, persuaded Baker to come to Punta Gorda in 1902. He had been born in Suwannee County, Florida, learned to read and write early in life, and became a teacher in north Florida. When he moved to Punta Gorda to teach, many people in the community came to admire him for his high ideals and hard work. After Baker died in 1942, officials built a school for African American children near his home and named it for him. Today it is used for preschool classes.

105. **Arnett Chapel A.M.E. Church** (Quincy in Gadsden County), at 209 South Duval Street, belongs to one of the oldest churches in the county, one that was organized in 1866, a year after the end of the Civil War. The building was constructed in 1938-39 and named for the Rev. Benjamin W. Arnett, the Presiding Bishop in Florida from 1888 to 1892.

106. **Hardon Building** (Quincy), at 16 W. Washington Street, was one of the town's earliest ice and electric plants and was owned by William Hardon, an African American. There was a bar in the front of the building, and a dice and card room was in the basement. The building, which was built around 1900, is now an office-supply business.

107. **Masonic Lodge** (Quincy), at 122 South Duval Street, has served as the Masonic Lodge meeting hall for African American masons since 1907. This simple, two-story building with an open hall on the first floor was moved from its original site in 1976 and remodeled.

108. **William S. Stevens Hospital** (Quincy), on the corner of Roberts and Crawford Streets, is now a private residence. Dr. William S. Stevens practiced medicine in Quincy for more than 50 years, through both the yellow fever outbreak of 1906 and the influenza epidemic of 1918. This two-story building was the hospital established by Dr. Stevens, who also had a clinic and a drugstore.

109. **Butler Beach** (St. Augustine in St. Johns County) on Anastasia Island, about eight miles south of St. Augustine on Highway A1A, was for many years the only beach African Americans were allowed to use between Jacksonville and Daytona Beach. In 1927, African American businessman Frank B. Butler (1885-1973) bought land between the Atlantic Ocean and the Matanzas River and developed it into Butler Beach. This politically active Floridian, who operated the Palace Market and College

Arnett Chapel A.M.E. Church
Florida State Archives

169

Park Realty in St. Augustine, is the subject of Barbara Walch's Book, *Frank B. Butler: Lincolnville Businessman and Founder of St. Augustine, Florida's Historic Black Beach* (St. Augustine: Rudolph Hadley, 1992).

110. Willie Galimore Community Center (St. Augustine), at 399 South Riberia Street, is a recreational facility named after Willie Galimore of St. Augustine. A man who played football for Florida A&M University and was named an All-American three times, Galimore went on to play professional football with the Chicago Bears for seven years and led the Bears in scoring in 1958. Phone: (904)824-5209.

111. Gracia Real de Santa Teresa de Mose (St. Augustine), located two miles north of St. Augustine off Highway A1A, was a place where slaves escaping from Georgia found safety more than 250 years ago. In 1738, the Spanish established Fort Mose (pronounced "Moh-say") and allowed escaping slaves to settle there if they became Catholics. That fort became the first free black community in North America. About 100 free black men, women, and children lived at the fort, farmed the fields, and helped the Spanish defend St. Augustine from the British. One reason the people of Fort Mose fought so hard was that they knew, if the British captured them, the British would make them slaves again. In 1763, when the British took control of Florida, the African Americans abandoned Fort Mose and went with the Spanish of St. Augustine to Cuba to begin new lives. Scientists have done some work at the site looking for material left by the free African Americans who lived there 250 years ago. Officials hope to create a place where visitors can see what life was like in such a fort so many years ago. See pp. 13-14.

112. Lincolnville Historic District (St. Augustine), which is in the middle of Cedar, Riberia, Cerro, and Washington Streets and DeSoto Place, used to be called "Africa" when former slaves began living there in 1866. Twenty years later Lincolnville was a growing community of African American businesses and homes. The district has the greatest concentration of late 19th-century architecture in the city.

113. St. Mary's Missionary Baptist Church (St. Augustine), at 69 Washington Street, is where Dr. Martin Luther King, Jr., told 300 supporters on June 9, 1964, that he would participate in a sit-in at a motel restaurant the next day. He was soon arrested, along with the white 72-year-old mother of the governor of Massachusetts. The publicity caused by these

Butler Beach Horse Patrol in the early 1950s
Florida State Archives

170

civil rights protests did much to influence Congress to pass the Civil Rights Act on June 20, 1964. See pp. 113-115. This Italian Gothic-style church was built in 1920.

114. **St. Paul's A.M.E. Church** (St. Augustine), at 85 Martin Luther King Avenue, is a 1910 Gothic Revival church which served as a gathering point for African Americans when they were fighting segregation in 1964. Baseball star Jackie Robinson spoke to the crowd here and encouraged them to continue on in their struggle.

115. **Cary A. White, Sr., Complex** (St. Augustine), at the Florida School for the Deaf and the Blind, 207 N. San Marco Avenue, is a classroom and dormitory area dedicated to the memory of the first African American deaf graduate of the school who worked there for 46 years. Mr. White worked in the dormitory where singer Ray Charles lived while he was a student there.

116. **Hopper Academy** (Sanford in Seminole County), at 1111 South Pine Avenue, is a two-story T-shaped building built between 1900 and 1910. It served as Sanford High School (Colored) and was one of the few early African American high schools in Florida. Local officials have plans to develop this facility into an educational and community service center.

117. **John M. Hurston House** (Sanford), at 621 East 6th Street, is a private residence once lived in by the Rev. John Hurston, the father of author/anthropologist Zora Neale Hurston. He and his wife, Mattie, lived in the house.

118. **St. James A.M.E. Church** (Sanford) at 819 Cypress Avenue is a red-brick building with four matching stained-glass windows. Built in 1913, the building is an excellent example of the work of African American architect Prince W. Spears. The congregation, which was organized in 1867, purchased the land on the corner of East 9th Street and South Cypress Avenue in 1880.

119. **Schoolhouse Gallery** (Sanibel Island in Lee County), at 520 Tarpon Bay Road, was a Baptist Church, built in 1909-1910, that also

Sanford: Hopper Academy
Kevin M. McCarthy

served as the only school for the African American children of the island in 1927. It remained that way until 1963, when Sanibel Elementary, the first integrated school in Lee County, was built. At the moment it serves as a gallery of fine art.

120. **Booker Schools** (Sarasota in Sarasota County) are commemorated by a historical marker at Orange Avenue and 35th Street. They were named for African American educator Emma E. Booker, who began teaching African American children in 1910 and eventually became principal of Sarasota Grammar School in 1918. She attended college during the summers for two decades in order to earn her bachelor's degree.

121. **First Black Community** (Sarasota) has a historical marker at Central Avenue between 5th and 6th Streets in Sarasota. Lewis Colson, the first African American settler in Sarasota, helped survey the town in 1886 and began what would become a prosperous African American residential and business district.

122. **Fort Gadsden State Historic Site** (near Sumatra in Franklin County), six miles southwest of Sumatra, off State Road 65, is the site of what was called the "Negro Fort." The British

built it, and African American and Native American forces under an African American commandant named Garcia used it. On June 27, 1816, under orders of President Andrew Jackson, the fort was attacked and destroyed, killing some 270 of the 320 defenders. Open 8 A.M.-sunset year-round. Phone: (904)670-8988. See pp. 15-16.

123. **Black Archives Research Center and Museum** (Tallahassee in Leon County), in the Carnegie Library Building at Florida A&M University, may be the largest collection of African American papers and items in the world. It is housed in the oldest building on campus, one that was built in 1907 and was the first library of its kind at an African American land-grant college. More than 100,000 visitors annually to the Center see such items as leg irons from a 17th-century slave ship, tribal masks, and ancient art from Africa, much of it collected by FAMU graduate Frank Pinder, who spent more than 30 years in Africa and India. Open 9 A.M. - 4 P.M., Monday-Friday. Phone: (904)599-3020.

124. **First Presbyterian Church** (Tallahassee), at 102 N. Adams Street, was built in 1838 and is the only church still standing in town from territorial days. Slaves were al-

Sarasota: Booker High School
Kevin M. McCarthy

172

lowed to be members of the church but had to sit in the north gallery apart from their masters.

125. Florida Agricultural and Mechanical University (Tallahassee) on South Adams Street is the oldest historically black university in Florida, having been established in 1887 as the Florida State Normal and Industrial School for Negroes. Its first president, Thomas DeSaille Tucker, was born in Sierra Leone and graduated from Oberlin College in 1886. He practiced law in Pensacola before arriving in Tallahassee in 1887. The Gallery of Distinction in the school's College of Education honors the state's great African American educators. See pp. 55-56.

126. Gibbs Cottage (Tallahassee) on South Adams Street, which was built in 1894, was the home of Thomas Van Renssalaer Gibbs, who served in the Florida Legislature and introduced in 1887 the bill which established the Florida State Normal and Industrial School for Negroes, now Florida A&M University.

127. Knott House (Tallahassee), at 301 East Park Avenue, was owned by Thomas and Catherine Hagner in 1865 during the Cival War

First Presbyterian Church, Tallahassee
Florida State Archives

when Union General Edward M. McCook made his headquarters there. On May 20th, McCook announced from the steps of the house President Lincoln's Emancipation Proclamation. The home, which was remodeled in the 1920s, is now a museum, with emphasis on the Knott family and the Depression years.

128. John G. Riley House (Tallahassee), at 419 West Jefferson Street, was the home that John Gilmore Riley built in the 1890s and lived in until he died in 1954. Riley was an African American educator and civic leader in Tallahassee in the late 19th and early 20th centuries who became the first principal of

Florida A&M Coleman Memorial Library
Florida State Archives

Reverend C. K. Steele
Florida State Archives

Lincoln Academy, the first high school for African Americans in Leon County.

129. St. James C.M.E. Church (Tallahassee), at 104 N. Bronough Street, which is now a private office, is the oldest African American church building still standing in Tallahassee. The church was built in 1899 on land bought by African American members of the Trinity Methodist Episcopal Church who formed a separate organization known as the Colored Methodist Episcopal Church. One of the earlier buildings on the same site may have been a hospital for wounded soldiers from the Civil War Battle of Olustee and later a school for African American children during Reconstruction after the Civil War.

130. C. K. Steele Memorial (Tallahassee), at 111 West Tennessee Street, consists of a statue and marker honoring the work of the Reverend Charles Kenzie Steele (1914-1980), one of Florida's outstanding civil rights leaders. Steele was pastor of Tallahassee's Bethel Baptist Church

and marched with Martin Luther King, Jr., in the 1950s and 1960s. He helped organize the Tallahassee bus boycott (see pp. 111-112) that succeeded in ending segregated seating on the buses. The new Tallahassee city bus terminal has his name and also a statue of this great man. See pp. 108-110.

131. Union Bank Building (Tallahassee), at the corner of Apalachee Parkway and Calhoun Street, one block from the Old Capitol, was chartered in 1833 and built in 1841. It may be Florida's oldest bank building. It has housed many cultural and business groups, including the National Freedman's Bank for newly freed slaves during Reconstruction after the Civil War and has been remodeled at least eight times. Open 10 A.M.-1 P.M., Tuesday-Friday; 1 P.M. - 4 P.M., weekends. Phone: (904) 487-3803.

132. La Union Marti-Maceo (Tampa in Hillsborough County) at 1226 E. 7th Avenue in the Ybor City National Historic Landmark District. This building has served Afro-Cubans who were excluded from other Cuban and Spanish clubs. Since it was established in 1904, the Marti-Maceo mutual aid society has helped many black Cubans in Ybor City who faced discrimination.

133. Museum of African American Art (Tampa), at 1308 Marion Street, has an excellent collection of African American art that shows the history, culture, and lifestyle of African Americans in America. It is also the oldest collection of African American art in the United States and has one piece dating from 1851. Open 10 A.M. - 4:30 P.M., Tuesday - Saturday; 1 P.M. - 4:30 P.M., Sunday (except holidays). Phone: (813)272-2466.

134. St. Paul A.M.E. Church (Tampa), at 506 East Harrison Street, served during the 1950s and 1960s as the place where civil rights leaders planned their protest against segregated restaurants in downtown Tampa. The building was constructed between 1906 and 1917.

135. **St. Peter Claver School** (Tampa), at 1401 Governor Street, is the oldest African American school, public or private, still operating in Hillsborough County. Ten days after it opened on February 2, 1894, it was destroyed by arson. Rebuilt and reopened, the school resumed classes under two Sisters of the Holy Names. Within seven years, its African American graduates were becoming certified teachers. In 1916, Governor Trammell issued a warrant for the arrest of three Sisters at another African American school, accusing them of violating an 1895 Florida law that outlawed whites teaching African Americans. Since St. Peter Claver School could be accused of violating the same law, its officials decided to close the school. When the law was later declared unconstitutional, the school reopened.

136. **Moss Hill United Methodist Church** (Vernon), three miles southeast of Vernon, off Vernon-Greenhead Road. Built in 1857 by church members and their slaves, this simple wood-frame church is the oldest such building in Washington County. Many of the planks still bear the hand- or fingerprints of the workers, and one can still see on the ceiling planks the barefooted imprints of children who walked on the planks before workers put up the ceiling. The building is one of the nation's best examples of frontier church architecture.

137. **Gwen Cherry House** (West Palm Beach in Palm Beach County), on the corner of 6th Street and Division Avenue, was the home of Gwendolyn Cherry, the first African American woman elected to the Florida Legislature.

The building will become a museum for the Black Historical Preservation Society of Palm Beach County.

138. **The Mickens House** (West Palm Beach), at 801 Fourth Street, is now a private residence. The house was built in 1917 by Halen Mickens, who worked at Colonel Bradley's casino. His widow, Alice Frederick Mickens, became famous for encouraging higher education for African Americans and was named "Outstanding Woman of the Century" at the American Negro Emancipation Convention in 1963. She entertained such important African Americans as Dr. Ralph Bunche, Mary McLeod Bethune, and A. Philip Randolph at her home.

139. **Northwest Neighborhood Historic District** (West Palm Beach) is bordered by N.W. 2nd and 11th Streets, North Rosemary and Douglas Avenues. The first African Americans came here between 1885 and 1890, when the African American residents of the area in Palm Beach known as the "Styx" were forced to relocate to the northwest section of the city. Local African American builders and contractors, for example, Simeon Mather, R. A. Smith, J. S. Woodside, Alfred Williams, and Samuel O. Major, built many of the buildings in the area. Local architects such as West Palm Beach's first African American architect, Hazel Augustus, and the firm of Harvey and Clarke, designed some of the buildings, especially churches. This district is the only part left of the original African American settlement.

140. **Tabernacle Baptist Church** (West Palm Beach), at 801 Eighth Street, was established in 1893 as Mount Olive Baptist Church. The church held classes for the first public school for African Americans in West Palm Beach

Stephen Foster Memorial, White Springs, Florida
Florida State Archives

from 1894 to 1896. This particular building was built in 1925.

141. **Stephen Foster State Folk Culture Center** (White Springs in Hamilton County), on U. S. Highway 41 North, 3 miles east of I-75, is a memorial to composer Stephen Foster. Located on the banks of the Suwannee River, this Center has an annual folk festival in which African American craftsmen participate. Park open 8 A.M. - sunset; buildings open 9 A.M. - 5 P.M. Phone: (904)397-2733.

GLOSSARY

abolitionists - people who wanted to get rid of slavery; in the United States abolitionists were particularly active before the Civil War.

accredited - officially approved.

act of secession - the law by which Southern states tried to withdraw from the Northern states in the mid-1800s. That law led to the American Civil War.

administration - a group of people in charge of operating something. Examples: a school administration, a city administration.

advocate - someone who speaks in favor of something or someone.

affordable housing - houses that people have enough money to buy.

African Methodist Episcopal Church - a church that African Americans established in the late 18th century in order for them to worship freely.

ancestors - relatives in the past.

anthropologist - a person who studies humanity. Anthropology is the study of humanity.

Apalachicola River - a river that flows into the Gulf of Mexico west of Tallahassee, Florida.

appeal - to have a case reheard in a higher court.

Army Air Corps - the aviation part of the United States Army.

artillery instructor - one who teaches others how to use large guns, like cannons.

attorney - a lawyer.

bar - the exam that a person must pass if he or she wants to become a lawyer. This exam is usually taken after finishing study at a law school.

barriers - things that block the way.

battlefield - the place where a battle is fought.

Bethune-Cookman College - a college established by Mary McLeod Bethune in Daytona Beach, Florida.

Black Archives Research Center and Museum - a special collection of material about African Americans in Florida; the center and museum are on the campus of Florida Agricultural and Mechanical University in Tallahassee.

Black Codes - laws that the Florida Legislature passed that tried to keep the former slaves down and in a new kind of slavery.

board of trustees - a group of people who manage a school, hospital, or some such organization.

bond - a written statement given by a government for a loan of money; when someone receives a bond, that person promises to repay the money borrowed and to pay it back on a certain date with interest.

booby trap - something that is meant to trick someone; a mine that is supposed to explode when someone picks it up. Soldiers will sometimes hide booby traps on paths or in the sand in hopes that the enemy soldiers will pick them up or stumble into them and be injured or killed by the traps.

boycott - to join other people in refusing to deal with a person, business, or nation.

braille - a system of printing that blind people can use to read. Braille uses raised dots for the letters of the alphabet; blind people can touch the dots with their fingers and understand what the letters are.

brain tumor - a group of cells in the brain that grow faster than normal cells.

brand - a mark made on the skin, often with a hot iron.

Brazil - a country in the central and northeastern part of South America. The Amazon River flows through Brazil.

budget - a plan for using money. A budget will show people how much money they will have and how they will spend it.

bust - a piece of sculpture showing only the head, shoulders, and chest.

cabinet - a group of official advisors to the head of a government.

campus - the buildings and grounds of a school.

cannonballs - heavy balls of metal or other metal that are used to attack forts.

Cape Florida Lighthouse - a lighthouse on Key Biscayne east of Miami.

carpenters - workers who build and repair wooden articles.

carpetbaggers - people who came to the South looking for ways to make money; they seemed to carry all of their clothes and articles in one piece of luggage (a carpet-bag), and that is why they were called carpetbaggers.

car pools - a system by which a group of people who ride together take turns at driving.

census - an official counting of the people who live in a city, state, or nation.

charges - statements that say that people have committed crimes; for example, "the police arrested the youth on charges of shoplifting."

Chief Justice - the judge in charge of other judges, for example on the Supreme Court of a state or nation.

City Council - a group of people who are elected to make laws for and help run a city.

civil rights - the rights of all the citizens of a country, for example the equal treatment of those people with respect to protection of the law.

Civil Rights Act - a law to guarantee the rights of people, especially minorities.

claims - demands for what people think is theirs; for example, after a disaster like a hurricane or a fire people will file claims with their insurance company to receive payment for what they lost.

coal miner - someone who takes coal from the ground, usually by digging.

color blind - not able to see the difference between certain colors; not influenced by considerations of race.

commission - a position of military rank; a group of persons who are chosen to do some special work, e.g. a city commission.

composer - one who writes music.

Confederate - referring to the Southern states during the American Civil War.

congressman - a man who is a member of the United States Congress in Washington, D.C.

congresswoman - a woman who is a member of the United States Congress in Washington, D.C.

constitution - the laws that control a state or country.

constitutional convention - a meeting that tries to draw up a way to organize a government.

constitutional rights - the powers and privileges that a constitution gives to a people.

consul - a person appointed by his/her government to live in a certain city in a foreign country and look after his/her country's citizens and business problems.

convert - to change from one religion to another.

convict-lease system - a method by which officials would rent out prisoners to people who would use them to work in turpentine camps or plantations or road-building crews, etc.

convicts - people who are serving a sentence in jail or prison.

correctional institution - a place where persons convicted of crimes spend their time as a punishment. Such a place is sometimes called a jail or a prison.

customhouses - the offices or buildings where officials clear ships for entering or leaving a port.

daughter-in-law - the wife of someone's son; for example, my son's wife is my daughter-in-law.

death row - the place in prison where condemned prisoners wait until they are executed.

debate - discussion or argument between two persons or groups. Many schools have debate teams that have contests with the debate teams of other schools.

delegate - a person who represents others at a meeting.

Department of Corrections - the part of government that controls prisons.

Depression - a time in the 1930s when businesses were not doing well, many people lost their jobs, and the country had a difficult time financially.

diploma - a printed piece of paper that a school gives to graduating students that says they have finished their studies at the school.

diplomat - someone who represents a government, especially in relation to another government.

disabled - crippled, handicapped.

disciplinarian - someone who believes in strict rules.

discrimination - the showing of hatred toward people because of their race or religion or country, etc.

dominate - to control because of power or importance.

economy - the money situation of a person or state.

editors - men and women who prepare written work for publication, for example in a newspaper or book.

educator - a teacher.

Edward Waters College - a college in Jacksonville that is the oldest independent institution of higher education in Florida.

electrocution - the killing of someone by a very strong electric shock.

Emancipation Proclamation- the freeing of some slaves by President Abraham Lincoln in 1863.

employment - work, jobs.

epidemic - a disease that makes many people in an area sick at the same time.

equality - the condition of being equal, for example in having the same rights and duties as others.

executive secretary - a person whose job it is to manage a school, business, or group.

fare - the cost of a ride on a bus, plane, ship, taxi, or train.

father-in-law - the father of someone's wife or husband; for example, my wife's father is my father-in-law.

federal circuit judge - a certain type of judge who works for the central government of the United States.

fever - a disease that makes the body very hot.

fiancé - a man to whom a woman is engaged to be married.

fighter pilot - someone who flies a small, light plane used in aerial combat.

finances - the money that a person, organization, or nation has.

flog - to beat with a whip.

Florida Black Heritage Trail - 141 sites around the state that are of importance in the history of African Americans in Florida.

Florida Legislature - a group of men and women who meet in Tallahassee each year and make laws for the state of Florida.

Florida Sports Hall of Fame - a building in Lake City, Florida, that features exhibits about Florida's sports heroes. (See #62 in the Florida Black Heritage Trail, p. 162.)

folklore - the beliefs, traditions, and customs of a people.

foreman - a person who is in charge of a group of workers.

freedmen - people who were legally freed from slavery.

ghetto - part of a city where members of a particular religion or race live because they are poor or because others discriminate against them.

gravestones - tombstones or stones placed over the graves with writing on them that tells about the dead persons.

Gulf Stream - a steady riverlike current of water in the Atlantic Ocean.

gunboats - small ships with weapons.

gunpowder - a powder used in rifles and cannons.

Haiti - a country on the island of Hispaniola in the West Indies.

hand grenades - small bombs that one can throw by hand.

Harlem Renaissance - a literary movement in New York City that produced many works by and about African Americans.

harvest - to gather in a crop.

historians - writers of history.

homeless - people who don't have a home.

honor court - an official gathering headed by a judge or judges that is to decide if certain laws have been broken. Many schools have honor courts to decide if students cheated in a test or copied someone else's work. Other students sit on the honor court and determine if the laws have been broken.

horticulture - the art or science of using land to grow vegetables, flowers, or other crops.

House of Representatives - part of the state's or country's legislature.

humanitarian - generous, kind, good.

Humphries, Frederick S. - president of Florida Agricultural and Mechanical University (FAMU) since 1985.

illiterate - not able to read or write.

injustice - unfairness.

insurance - a system of protection against loss; people pay a certain amount of money to guarantee that they or their family will receive money in case of an accident or fire or death.

interpreters - people who translate a foreign language for those who do not know that foreign language.

ironsmiths - men and women who work with iron.

Jackson, Andrew - an American general and the seventh U.S. president.

Jamaica - a country on an island in the West Indies south of Cuba.

Jim Crow laws - laws that discriminated against African Americans.

justice - a judge on the Supreme Court of a state or country; fair or right treatment.

Key Biscayne - an island east of Miami.

Key West - a town in the Florida Keys at the end of Highway U.S. 1.

klansmen - members of a group like the Ku Klux Klan.

Ku Klux Klan - a secret society of white people that persecutes African Americans.

land battle - a large fight on land between forces from different sides of a war.

Lewey, Matthew M. - the man who established one of the state's more famous African American newspapers, the *Sentinel*, in Gainesville in 1887.

liberal arts - college courses such as literature, philosophy, history, and languages.

lieutenant governor - an elected official of a state who performs the duties of the governor when the governor is away or sick or dead.

lynch - to kill someone without a lawful trial, usually by hanging.

machine gunner - someone who fires a gun that keeps rapidly firing bullets as long as the person is pressing the trigger. Such a gun is called a machine gun.

Madagascar - a large island in the Indian Ocean off the southeastern coast of Africa.

magistrate - a person whose job it is to administer and enforce the law.

major league teams - the main teams of professional baseball clubs in the United States.

martyr - someone who chooses to suffer or die rather than give up what they believe in.

mast - a tall pole that goes up from the deck of a boat and supports the sails.

mayor - the chief administrative officer of a town or city.

Medal of Honor - a flat piece of metal, also called the Congressional Medal of Honor, which is given to those brave soldiers who risked their lives to help others.

memorial - something that reminds us of people or events. Monuments and statues can be memorials.

miller - a person who owns or operates a mill, for example a flour mill.

missionaries - persons sent out by a church or organization to preach and teach.

Morocco - a country in the northwest part of Africa.

National Association for the Advancement of Colored People - (NAACP) - an organization, which was established in 1910 and whose goal is to end racial discrimination and segregation of African Americans. It has supported nonviolent protests against discrimination. Its early efforts were directed against lynching. Since World War II it has worked more and more toward integration, especially of schools.

Negro Leagues - groups of African American baseball teams that were not allowed to play in the white leagues.

nonviolent - peaceful.

obstacles - things or people that stand in the way and block progress.

officials - men and women who serve the public in office, for example mayors and governors.

orphanage - a place where orphans live.

outhouse - an outdoor toilet usually consisting of a small building separate from, but located near, the main house.

outlaw - to declare to be illegal. A criminal.

Pascua Florida - a phrase that means "Feast of Flowers" in Spanish.

pastor - the minister in charge of a church.

180

pavilion -part of a building.

physicians - medical doctors.

plantations - areas for growing crops, for example sugar plantations.

plead - to argue or defend.

political science - the study of how a government works, how it is organized, what runs it.

politician - a person who holds or tries to win a government office.

polls - a place where people vote.

population - the number of people who live somewhere.

postmaster - the person in charge of a post office.

potter -someone who makes pots, dishes, and other objects from clay.

pottery - the art of making pots, dishes, and other objects from clay.

poverty - the condition of being poor.

prejudice - hatred or unfair treatment of people.

prisons - jails where prisoners or soldiers from the enemy side are kept.

probation - a period of time in which a person's ability or behavior is tested. When a judge puts people on probation, they are allowed to remain out of jail as long as they promise to keep out of trouble. They usually have to check in with a probation officer who makes sure they are keeping out of trouble.

public defender - someone who defends people, often at no expense to the people, accused of a crime. Public defenders often defend poor people who cannot afford a lawyer.

qualification - something that makes a person fit for a job.

race relations - the connections or dealings between different races.

racism - the practice of discrimination against people because of their race.

Reconstruction - the time in the United States after the Civil War when the Nation began to heal itself.

reef - a line of rocks just below the surface of the water; ships sometimes crash into reefs and sink.

reforms - changes for the better.

retreat - to move back, for example from a battle.

role model - someone who is worthy enough to be imitated by others.

salary - a fixed amount of money that is paid to someone for work.

sap - the juice or liquid that goes through a plant or tree.

sawmill - a place where workers use machines to cut trees or logs into lumber.

scholarly - having a great deal of knowledge.

scholarship - a gift of money or other aid to help students continue their studies.

scouts - persons sent out to learn information, for example about an enemy.

sculptor - a person who carves figures from clay, stone, metal, or wood.

sculptures - any carved objects, for example statues and figures, from clay, stone, metal, or wood.

secede - to leave an organization like a nation.

Second Seminole War - a war that federal troops fought against the Seminole Native Americans in Florida from 1835 until 1841.

secretary of state - the person in charge of that part of state or national government which handles many important duties of the government, for example relations with other states or governments.

segregation - the act of separating or keeping apart, for example those of different races.

self-reliant - trusting one's own abilities.

seminary - a school that trains students to be ministers, priests, or rabbis.

Seminole Wars - wars between the federal government and the Seminole Tribes in Florida in the 1800s.

Seminoles - Florida Native Americans who fought against the U.S. government in the Second Seminole War. Many Seminoles live in Florida and Oklahoma today.

shackles - metal fasteners that kept prisoners or slaves tied up.

Sierra Leone - a country in west Africa on the Atlantic Ocean.

slave - a human being who is owned by another human being.

slavery - the owning or keeping of slaves.

slums - a crowded area in which housing and other living conditions are very poor.

slur - something that is said to hurt someone else.

smuggle - to bring something secretly into a country.

smugglers - those who bring something secretly

into a country.

social worker - one who performs work that will help a community, for example through health clinics and recreation halls.

sophomore - a student in the second year of a four-year school.

squad - a small group of soldiers who work or fight together.

St. Petersburg - a city on the west coast of Florida.

state legislator - a person who makes or passes state laws.

state superintendent of public instruction - the person in charge of a state's schools.

state supervisor of elections - the person who watches over and directs the elections of a state.

state treasurer - a person who is in charge of the money of a state.

steamboats - boats that are powered by steam.

Stowe, Harriet Beecher - the woman who wrote *Uncle Tom's Cabin.*

strawberry schools - schools that were open in the summer but closed in the winter, at which time students were expected to pick strawberries and other crops in the fields.

stroke - a sudden attack, usually loss of consciousness, caused by a problem with an artery in the brain.

suit - a case that is brought to a court of law.

superintendent of schools - the person in charge of operating a school system.

sweatbox - a small box that had no light and no air going through it; prisoners were put in such a box as a form of punishment.

Tallahassee - a city in north Florida that is now the capital of the state.

Tampa Bay - a large body of water near the city of Tampa.

tanner - someone who changes the skin of animals into leather.

tenant farmers - farmers who pay money to use land that belongs to someone else.

thrifty - careful in using money.

ties - something which connects or joins; example: "She has close ties with her high school friends."

torture - to cause a person to suffer great pain.

track meets - contests where athletes compete in such sports as running.

trail blazer - a pioneer in a field.

trial - the examination in a court of law of people accused of a crime.

trio - a group of three things or persons.

tuberculosis - an infectious disease that can affect the lungs.

tuition - money that is paid for teaching.

turpentine - a liquid that one mixes with paints to make them thinner.

turpentine camps - camps in which workers make turpentine.

type - a small block of metal or wood that has a letter of the alphabet on one end; printers used to use these blocks to print newspapers.

unaccredited - not officially approved.

Underground Railroad - a way that abolitionists used to help runaway slaves in the South escape to Canada and the free states of the North.

Union - the Northern states during the American Civil War.

Union Academy - a school established by the Freedmen's Bureau in Gainesville in 1866.

unskilled workers - workers who have no special skill or training.

varsity letter - the initial of a school that is given to a student as an award. For example, usually a school will give varsity letters to the school's best athletes.

vertebra - one of the small bones in a person's backbone.

veterinarian - a doctor who treats animals.

voter registration - the placing of one's name on a list of people allowed to vote.

wage - money paid for work that is done.

warrant - an official paper that allows the police to arrest or search someone.

waterspout - a fast-moving column of air that goes from a storm cloud down to the water.

white supremacists - people who believe that white people should have the highest authority and power.

will - a legal document containing a person's wishes about his or her property after death.

wing - part of a building that sticks out from the main part of the building.

witnesses - people who have seen or heard something.

INDEX

183

INDEX